The History & Use of Amulets, Charms and Talismans

Gary R. Varner

The History & Use of Amulets, Charms and Talismans

Copyright © 2008 by Gary R. Varner

All rights reserved. No part of this publication may be reproduced, stored in a retrieval system, or transmitted, in any form, or by any means, without the prior permission of the copyright holder.

ISBN: 978-1-4357-1988-0 (paperback)
978-0-557-00891-9 (hardcover)

An OakChylde Book
Published by Lulu Press, Inc.
Visit the author's website: www.authorsden.com/garyrvarner

Unless otherwise indicated, all photographs in this work were taken by the author. The image on the title page is that of an "abraxas" amulet. An interesting image similar to the serpent-legged Titans is carved upon the strange "Abrasax gems," magical amulets introduced in the second century that mingled early Christian and Pagan themes. Originating in Alexandria, the images most certainly were inspired by the mystic powers of the man-serpent as represented by the Titans.

Amulet, n. an ornament or small piece of jewelry worn as a protection against evil. – *Oxford Dictionary of Current English, 4th edition.*

Charm. n. an object, act, or saying believed to have magic power. – *Oxford Dictionary of Current English, 4th edition.*

An amulet…is anything hung around the neck, placed like a bracelet on the wrist, or otherwise attached to the person, as an imagined preservative against sickness or other evils; a charm is exactly the same thing, the only difference being the word itself contains the notion of some human action imparting to the article a certain power for good…a talisman is a special kind of charm on which is engraved a magical figure, worn to avoid disaster to the wearer." –T. Sharper Knowlson, *The Origins of Popular Superstitions and Customs* (1930)

The History & Use of Amulets, Charms and Talismans

Gary R. Varner

Contents

Introduction		6
I.	Amulets & Charms through time	9
II.	The use of magic in Christianity	28
III.	Amulets in Witchcraft & Sorcery	35
IV.	Animal Totems	51
V.	Native American use of amulets	104
VI.	Charms	111
VII.	Stones as Amulets and Charms	119
VIII.	Amulets for Health	156
IX.	Contemporary use of charms	161
Afterword		173
Bibliography		174
Index		182
About the Author		189

The History & Use of Amulets, Charms and Talismans

Introduction

Amulets and charms have been used since mankind evolved from its distant ancestry millions of years ago. They have been used to protect and to harm, and in both the practice and avoidance of witchcraft and sorcery. They are made of wood and stone, clay, metal, plants and dead animals. They are carved into crude shapes and in the most exquisite forms. They are also comprised entirely of words, which are believed to have power and magical properties.

Amulets and charms have been used by pagans, Christians, Jews and followers of every faith and tradition known across the world. Some are considered direct links to the gods, others to local spirits. All are links to the supernatural.

Unfortunately, the terms "amulets," "charms" and "talismans" have been used interchangeably even though each one stands alone. The best definition that I have seen was written by Sheila Paine who said "An amulet is a device, the purpose of which is to protect, but by magical and not physical means—a lump of meteorite worn against gunfire is an amulet, a bullet-proof vest is not.

"A charm is something believed to bring good luck, health and happiness…but protection is not its primary function.

"A talisman is something thought to be imbued with some magical property. It can both protect, and radiate power, and is often used in ritual." [1]

Regardless if they are called amulets, charms or talismans, these objects are credited with cures, evil spells, health and

---

[1] Paine, Sheila. *Amulets: Sacred Charms of Power and Protection.* Rochester: Inner Traditions 2004, 10.

prosperity. This book will explore the history, use and folklore concerning amulets and will show that amulets continue to be an important part of our modern culture.

I
Amulets & Charms through Time

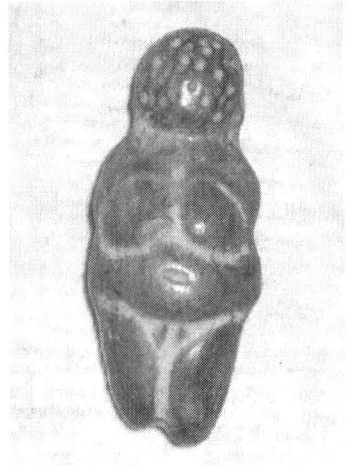

Amulets have been worn by men, women and children for thousands of years and continue to be a fashion accessory today. One of the most famous is the "Venus of Willendorf" found in Austria and dated to 30,000 BCE. However, they have been subject to Christian disfavor also due to their ancient pagan history. In 355 CE the Council of Laodicea decreed that priests and clerks "must be neither enchanters, mathematicians, nor astrologers, and they must not make 'what are called amulets,' for these were fetters of the soul, and all who wore them should be cast out of the church." [2] It should be noted that mathematics was included not as a mistake, but as a way to "protect" the Church against intellectual reason and knowledge, which the Church fairly accomplished during the Dark Ages.

Amulets, usually short spells written on small pieces of papyrus and rolled into cylindrical tubes, were commonly worn around the neck as a form of protection. These tubes have been found dating from 1100 BCE [3] to 747 BCE, during the late New Kingdom and the Third Intermediate Period of Egypt.

---

[2] Kunz, George Frederick. *The Curious Lore of Precious Stones*. New York: Dover Publications, Inc. 1971, 42-43.
[3] BCE=Before Common Era

"The text usually read as if it were a proclamation by a deity or the gods in general, promising to protect the wearer and threatening divine retribution to those who endangered him or her." [4]

Apparently, children were most likely to wear these amulets to protect them from the Evil Eye, demons, sorcerers, and other harm.

The sorcerer in Iceland, Kieckhefer tells us, "is a specialist who performs services for others. She deploys ceremonies and magically charged objects, but her main source of power is the spoken and written word..."[5] But in Icelandic society magic and sorcery are considered reprehensible, not, as Kieckhefer relates, because it is violent but because it is "unfair." Disputes were handled by hand-to-hand combat, not by magic spells from afar.

As in most cultures, the Icelandic witch was usually an old woman with certain special knowledge but she was not an outcast of society nor was she viewed as anything other than an old woman. While magic was considered unsavory, "it is almost always a means for confronting or evading one's enemies." [6]

Spells were cast with caution—especially if a magician threatened or attempted to coerce a demon or malignant power through the spell. In these cases, the sorcerer always attributed the spell to a much higher power or god. "It is Isis who says it,' or 'I am Re in this his mysterious name." [7]

---

[4] Oakes, Lorna and Lucia Gahlin. *Ancient Egypt.* New York: Barnes & Noble, Inc. 2006, 455.
[5] Kieckhefer, Richard. *Magic in the Middle Ages.* Cambridge: Cambridge University Press 1989, 50.
[6] Ibid.
[7] James, E. O. James, E.O. *The Ancient Gods.* Edison: Castle Books 2004, 239.

Gary R. Varner

The Evil Eye

The "evil eye" is perhaps the most ancient form of hex that is still in use today. Thirteenth-century English Franciscan and scholar Robert Grosseteste wrote:

> "'Casting the evil eye' is when someone who is filled with envy infects by a glance or by words of praise someone of tender age, someone born recently, and changes what is perfect into something which is worse: like the Devil who first envied Man and by his jealousy opened the door for death to enter the world.
>
> "But whether the Evil Eye as the common people understand it is something else or not, I cannot easily say. For who knows whether an envious person's sight is poisonous and infects those of tender years, as the sight of a basilisk infects the air and anything it looks at, and as the sight of a menstruating woman infects a new mirror, freshly cleaned and polished?" [8]

Witches and warlocks who practiced the evil eye were greatly feared in ancient Babylon and there are a few references to it in the Old Testament. Proverbs 6:12-14 describes such a person:

"…a wicked man walketh with a forward mouth. He winketh with his eyes, he speaketh with his feet, he teacheth with his fingers. Forwardness is in his heart, he deviseth mishief continually, he soweth discord."

Proverbs 23:6 cautioned, "Eat thou not the bread of him that hath an evil eye…"

---

[8] "The Evil Eye: Expositio in epistolam Sancti Pauli ad Galatas" in *The Occult in Mediaeval Europe* edited and translated by P.G. Maxwell-Stuart. Hampshire: Palgrave MacMillan 2005, 38

Evil eye was recorded by the ancient Egyptians, Sumerians and throughout the Greco-Roman world; but it is also found in every European nation, Mexico, Africa and South America , as well as in the mythology of India.

Jacqueline Simpson noted, "There is such similarity between classical sources and recent folklore about the nature and effects of the evil eye, and even what amulets, words, and gestures to use against it, that one can safely assume continuity of tradition across the centuries." [9]

The evil eye was regarded as a form of "mental fire" in Indian mythology. According to Hopkins, "There are other fires, of knowledge...of the curse...and above all of the eye, which can burn. Even Gāndhārī, when she looks at Yudhiṣṭhira, raises a blister on his finger." [10]

One of the characters in the Indian epics, Nahuṣa, a seer who "always has the poison-look", was said to possess the evil eye that "absorbed power from all he saw." [11] Nahuṣa's evil eye was so feared by the other gods that they conspired to do away with him.

C.J.S. Thompson, writing in 1932, said, "the 'evil eye,' as it came to be termed, has ever been the most dreaded vehicle of spiritual malice." [12]

In 1352, eight individuals accused of killing children with the evil eye were sent to the stake by the Inquisition in Toulouse, France. [13] This form of evil magic was recorded over a thousand years earlier in ancient Mesopotamia but was

---

[9] Simpson, Jacqueline. "Evil eye" in *Medieval Folklore*. Oxford: Oxford University Press 2002, 122.
[10] Hopkins, E. Washburn. *Epic Mythology*. Delhi: Motilal Banarsidass 1986, 99.
[11] Ibid., 131
[12] Thompson, C.J.S. *The Hand of Destiny: Everyday Folklore and Superstitions.* London: Senate 1995, 65.
[13] Russell, Jeffrey Burton. *Witchcraft in the Middle Ages.* Ithaca: Cornell University Press 1972, 185.

treated somewhat differently. According to Thomsen, "the evil eye brought rather harmless, everyday accidents; a tool or pot was broken, clothes were torn, food was spoiled and the like. This might be serious and annoying...but as a rule it did not require complicated and expensive rituals or the assistance of an exorcist...Protection was, for instance, given by amulets, i.e. certain stones, probably in eye shape." [14] In fact, many amulets were easily utilized. Mackenzie tells us "Shells protected wearers against evil, including the evil eye." [15]

Children and fine livestock were often the victims of evil eye. Cows would experience a loss of milk and a "frantic wildness which usually resulted in collapse. Horses afflicted by the evil eye would sweat and tremble and grow weaker daily." [16]

Preventative charms used for the protection of cattle and horses included the use of rowan, juniper, horseshoes, burning cloth, tar, string charms, and iron among others.

According to Spence, "An Orkney witch, Catherine Grant, who was alive and mischievous in 1623, was observed to look over her shoulder and turn up the white of her eye...The effects were often instantaneous. Ale and milk could be turned sour by such a glance." [17]

Early historians such as Pliny and Cicero reported that the evil eye was capable of killing anyone who was stared at. Thomas Aquinas supposedly referred to old women who could harm children simply by looking at them.

---

[14] Thomsen, Marie-Louise. "Witchcraft and Magic in Ancient Mesopotamia" in *Witchcraft and Magic in Europe: Biblical and Pagan Societies.* Philadelphia: University of Pennsylvania Press 2001, 42-43.
[15] Mackenzie, Donald A. *Ancient Man in Britain.* London: Senate 1996, 39.
[16] Spence, Lewis. *The Magic Arts in Celtic Britain.* Mineola: Dover Publications, Inc. 1999, 62.
[17] Ibid., 63.

The infamous sheela-na-gig, a grotesque carving of a emaciated and bald woman with genitals widely displayed found on ancient cathedrals, churches and castles may have been created as a means to avert the evil eye and other black forces. "As 'fertility' symbols they have the power to turn aside the forces of evil, the maleficent glance of the Evil Eye." [18]

Celtic scholar Anne Ross wrote "Rowan was held to be a potent talisman against the Evil Eye (in Scotland); and even today, there are extant, charms and incantations to counter the effects of the 'eye.'" Other methods used to counteract the evil eye malady included hanging iron horseshoes and utilizing certain plants and stones. In addition, Ross informs us, "It could also be averted by drinking three mouthfuls of water which had been poured over silver; each mouthful must be taken in the name of the Trinity." [19]

A certain illnesses in Spain and Mexico, *mal de ojo*, or evil eye, is said to be caused by individuals who have the ability, even an involuntary ability, to "impose illness merely by gazing fixedly at another person." [20] Children are most susceptible to this magic and if left untreated or not treated early enough, it is said to turn into a terminal illness.

Only a "curandero" can understand and possibly cure *mal de ojo*. A curandero is a witch-healer but contrary to their European counterparts, the curandero is considered a holy person in the service of God.

---

[18] Weir, Anthony and James Jerman. *Images of Lust: Sexual Carvings on Medieval Churches.* London: Routledge 1993, 10.
[19] Ross, Anne. *Folklore of the Scottish Highlands.* Gloucestershire: Tempus Publishing Ltd.2000, 82.
[20] Granger, Byrd Howell. "Some Aspects of Folk Medicine among Spanish-speaking People in Southern Arizona" in *American Folk Medicine A Symposium.* Berkeley: University of California Press 1976, 196.

To the Ethiopian Qemant the evil eye is certainly indicative of witchcraft and part of psychic projections that can be injurious. Usually the evil eye is used by persons desiring the property of another. "In most instances," writes anthropologist Frederick Gamst, "the evil-eyed person is said to be from an ethnic group other than one's own, but it is possible for a witch to be found within one's own group." [21]

The Qemant claimed that their neighboring group, the Falasha "are thought to have the evil eye and to turn nocturnally into hyenas which devour human corpses, especially victims of evil eye..."[22]

An age-old practice of Qemant women is to prepare food in the dark corners of their home in the attempt to avoid evil eye pollution from strangers.

A particular form of evil eye, called "eye piercing" can be done by anyone in Qemant society. This is accomplished by looking at a person with "strong envy", the envy conveyed by thought only. Gamst notes, "almost anyone can project witchlike qualities at times." [23]

William de Blécourt points out that "there is little in the descriptions of the evil eye that justifies its separation from witchcraft in general"[24] and along with the use of fetishes, evil eye is a main category of bewitchment.

This is somewhat simplistic, however, as a fair amount of anecdotal information over the years indicates that many

---

[21] Gamst, Frederick C. *The Qemant: A Pagan-Hebraic Peasantry of Ethiopia.* New York: Holt, Rinehart and Winston Case Studies in Cultural Anthropology 1969, 53.
[22] Ibid.
[23] Ibid., 54.
[24] Blécourt, William de. "The Witch, her Victim, the Unwitcher and the Researcher: The Continued Existence of Traditional Witchcraft" in *Witchcraft and Magic in Europe: The Twentieth Century*. Philadelphia: University of Pennsylvania Press 1999, 196.

persons capable of the evil eye had no control over it or even recognized that they could use such a power. While evil eye is directly associated with envy, it would seem unlikely that envy would play into the situation if the individual had no concept that he was directing an evil eye towards another individual. In addition, there are examples of people with the evil eye who attempted at least to take great pains not to harm anyone. Two examples of this are reported in Simpson and Roud: "there is an account from Yorkshire of a man who kept his eyes fixed on the ground so as not to harm anyone, and another who made sure he looked at a pear tree first thing every morning so that it would take the brunt of his power." [25]

In fact, writers in the 16th and 17th centuries suggested that the evil eye was the result of "certain harmful properties in the eye or in other parts of the body of certain types of people. It could not always be considered a result of ill-will on their part." [26]

Spanish priest Fray Martin de Castañega wrote in the 16th century "the 'evil eye' is a natural phenomenon and the result of the foul thoughts and evil designs which shine through certain people's eyes—more particularly through those of elderly spinsters, cripples, and certain types of sick people." [27] Thompson elaborates this point, saying "hunchbacks, dwarfs, deformed or people with squinting or different coloured eyes are also regarded as possessors of the power..." [28] Thompson also notes that women were considered the most capable of the evil eye.

---

[25] Simpson, Jacqueline and Steve Roud. *Oxford Dictionary of English Folklore.* Oxford: Oxford University Press 2000, 113.
[26] Baroja, Julio Caro. *The World of the Witches.* London: Phoenix Press 2001, 132.
[27] Ibid.
[28] Thompson, op cit., 66.

Again we see the common denominator in who was most likely to be accused of witchcraft—the elderly, the crippled, women and the sick, all most likely poor.

Various amulets were utilized since ancient times to ward off the evil eye and its effects. In Egypt, the "Eye of Horus" symbol was worn by both the living and the dead. This amulet was also used by the Romans, Etruscans and Greeks. Others include a sprig of rue, charms in the shape of the moon, crescent, horns, dogs, pigs, wheels, ladders, hooks, frogs, snails, lions, lizards, hands, clubs, knives and serpents.

Phallic talismans were used by the ancient Romans to ward off the evil eye and were worn around the neck by children who were always more susceptible to the ill-effects of the evil eye.

"In southern Italy," wrote Thompson, "where belief in the 'evil eye' still persists, the use of garlic or even the word that signifies that odorous bulb, is considered a sovereign preventative…" [29]

Various folk-medicine preventions and treatments continue to exist in the United States for the evil eye. In Los Angeles, it was recorded that "to ward off the evil eye from a child, make certain to always include some item of red in his attire." [30] This was especially effective in protecting a "beautiful child" from evil. Traditionally children, especially "beautiful children," have always been more at risk to suffer the effects of the evil eye. Thompson believed that this fear concerning "beautiful children" may have been a result of strangers noticing "pretty children" more than other children. While the color red was recommended in Los Angeles, in

---

[29] Ibid., 70.
[30] UCLA Folklore Archives Record Number 1_5369

Ohio in 1955 it was said, "wear blue and the evil eye won't get you." [31]

Water also figured into various folk treatments. The following is a rather complex treatment from California:

"If someone looks at your child with the evil eye, the child will get feverish and sick. Put a little bit of water in a cup and break an egg into it. Then put two straws crosswise in the form of a cross in the cup. Put the cup under the child's bed and pray the 'Credo'. The next day the egg has turned white.

"Go to the crossroads and throw it into the middle. This will cure the child." [32]

A similar method (recorded in Ohio in 1956) suggests that one should "put water in a dish and hold it over the person's head. Make a cross in the water with oil, and the curse will go away." [33]

Methods that are even more cumbersome were practiced in the "northern countries." "It was customary for a woman," wrote Thompson, to 'take off her shift over her head, turn herself around three times from right to left, then, while holding the garment open, to drop a burning coal through it three times before putting it on again." [34] This probably was a boon to the local dry goods merchant.

Folklore also indicates what type of person is the most likely to utilize the evil eye. A bit of Jewish lore from California said "Jews are afraid to let a gentile look at a newborn baby for fear it will receive the 'evil eye,' and a tradition among Italians in 1950s Ohio appears to recall the 16th century writings of Fray Castañega, "deformed people, usually older ones, have the evil eye." [35]

---

[31] UCLA Folklore Archives Record Number 1_5140
[32] UCLA Folklore Archives Record Number 1_6153
[33] UCLA Folklore Archives Record Number 1_5142
[34] Thompson, op cit., 74.
[35] UCLA Folklore Archives Record Number 1_5137

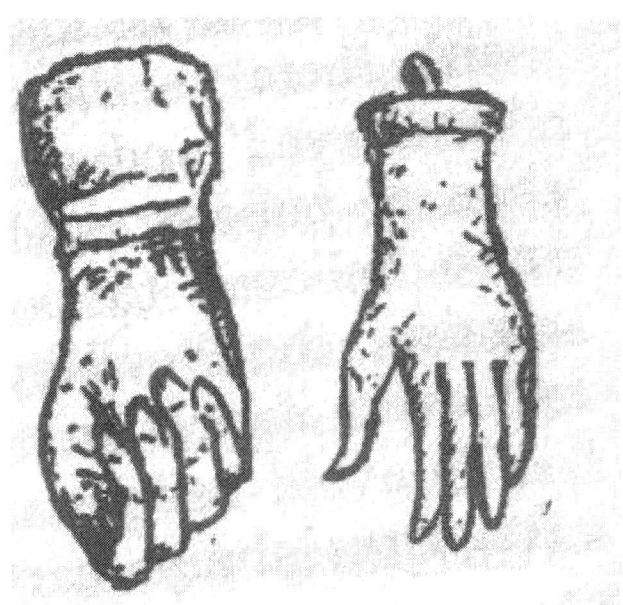

Egyptian hand charms used to avert the "Evil Eye." Circa 1500 BCE. From *The Hand of Destiny* by C.J.S. Thompson, published by Rider & Company, London 1932.

Another tool used to combat the evil eye was the "witch ball." Similar to the "disco balls" of the 1980s, these large glass balls were coated with a glossy reflecting paint of silver, gold or other bright colors. First created around 1690, they were hung in the window and were supposed to attract and neutralize the evil eye and reflect it back on the witch. It was also referred to as a "watch ball" as it would grow dull "if there is infection in the air" which served as a warning to the owner. [36]

Strangely enough, many of the folk methods used to prevent the effects of evil eye imply that anyone and everyone could cast it. Lady Wilde cautioned, "Never take an infant in

---

[36] Simpson and Roud, op cit., 394.

your arms, nor turn your head to look at it without saying, 'God bless it.' This keeps away the fatal influence of the Evil Eye." [37] However, she does seem to fix the real source of the evil eye on unbaptized children: "such generally grow up evil and have the evil eye, and bring ill luck, unless the name of God is instantly invoked when they look at any one fixedly and in silence." [38] In addition she states that children born at Whitsuntide (an English term for Pentecost) "are foredoomed, they will either have the evil eye, or commit murder, or die a violent death." [39]

The Evil Eye continues to cause fear and retribution in our contemporary society. Gang members in particular have killed individuals for the "hard stares" they believe were directed toward them.

Charms

Charms have been used around the world for luck, avoidance of evil, and for prosperity. Many charms take the form of amulets to be worn or carried on the person. Others are written, spoken or sung. Luck noted "Magical spells were often sung or chanted, and it was thought that the music — in itself a kind of magic, *thelxis* — added to the power of the works and acts. In Latin, *Carmen* means 'song' and 'spell'. The English words 'charming' and enchanting' still reflect these ancient beliefs." [40] In this context charms originally referred to

---

[37] Wilde, Lady. *Irish Cures, Mystic Charms & Superstitions.* New York: Sterling Publishing Co., Inc. 1991, 62.
[38] Ibid., 104.
[39] Ibid., 115.
[40] Luck, George. "Witches and Sorcerers in Classical Literature" in *Witchcraft and Magic in Europe: Ancient Greece and Rome.* Philadelphia: University of Pennsylvania Press 1999, 99.

oral formulas but in modern times the term has come to mean a variety of things, mostly worn or carried.

As indicated previously, during the early Christian period magic was a daily practice, not only by the common person, but also by the priests and administrators of the Church. "Priests provided amulets and charms," Luck wrote, "for the faithful, and a fifth-century Bishop was very familiar with pagan magic." [41]

As part of Gregory the Greats (590-604 CE) instructions to his monks and priests to preserve pagan temples and festivals but to give them Christian names and functions, monks who traveled about often would find pagan charms. They would write the formulas and names of any gods that were contained on them to record their journeys so that Christian versions of them could be made.

Charms many times took on the form of commands. Kieckhefer reports one 14th century example used on plants,: "In the name of Christ, amen, I conjure you, O herb, that I may conquer by Lord Peter…by the moon and stars…and may you conquer all my enemies, pontiffs and priests and all laymen and all women and all lawyers who are working against me…" [42]

Generally speaking, all verbal formulas spoken for good luck and good health are classified as charms. Healing charms originating from medieval times were called, by their practitioners, "blessings." These charms were normally whispered and accompanied by the sign of the cross, spitting or breathing on an ill person, or rubbing him or her with various colored cloths.

An early ethnological account of charms used in Sri Lanka, formerly known as Ceylon, illustrates the use of words as a

---

[41] Ibid., 158.
[42] Kieckhefer, op cit., 84.

form of powerful medicinal spell-work. As will be seen, the author is very ethnocentric in his remarks:

> No undertaking of any kind is attempted by the Singalese without invoking the aid of some supernatural power...This, no doubt, is the result of the teaching of a religion in itself inert and lifeless. Accordingly, when assailed by disease, the Singalese resort to supernatural aid, and hence *the treatment of diseases by charms.*
>
> "A charm, among the Singalese, is the pronouncing of a set form of words, either in Sanskrit or any other learned language, unintelligible to the masses, in which the *God* or *Yakko*, who presides over the particular malady is evoked. Persons suffering from colic, toothache, fever, snake-bites, etc., among the lower classes, frequently resort to have a charm pronounced over them... [43]

"Medieval and Elizabethan charms," noted Simpson and Roud, "made copious use of names of God, Jesus, and angels, in garbled Latin, Greek or Hebrew, plus scraps of Biblical quotations, usually in Latin. Some seemingly gibberish words, such as AGLA, were acronyms for religious phrases—in this case, for the Hebrew for 'Thou art powerful and eternal, O Lord'—though the users probably did not know it." [44]

Some charms use the "word-square" that utilizes the same word arranged in a square, the word reading the same forwards and backwards, vertically and horizontally. While many of these have been found from Christian times there are a number as well that have been discovered in Pompeii,

---

[43] Dickman, Henry. "Treatment of Diseases by Charms as practiced by the Singalese in Ceylon" in *Transactions of the Ethnological Society of London, Vol. II*. London: John Murray 1863, 142.

[44] Simpson, Jacqueline & Steve Roud. *Oxford Dictionary of English Folklore*. Oxford: Oxford University Press 2000, 57.

Portugal and along the Euphrates dating from the pre-Christian era.

"There is no doubt," wrote archeologist Ralph Merrifield, "that the word-square had a strong appeal as an emblem of mystery and power, and it was probably used as a magical spell from the beginning. It has survived in that capacity to our own times." [45]

Many magical charms were used to counter witchcraft, the horseshoe is one of these, being a specific antidote to witchcraft. The continued use of horseshoes as "lucky charms" is a direct survival of this belief. The intentional burial of iron tools and knives in house walls is another practice that is relatively recent.

Other anti-witchcraft charms include the "witch bottle." These items were used well into the 18th century and normally included bent pins, human hair and nail clippings, and pieces of cloth sometimes in the shape of a heart. These witch bottles were intended as counter-measures to witchcraft and were usually buried under the threshold or hearth of a home. [46]

That charms and incantations were continually used by the general populace for such mundane things as cooking is illustrated in the following item contained in the August 22, 1857 issue of the British journal, *Notes and Queries:*

> A gentleman whose name is well known to the public, and who has gained a deservedly high reputation in the photographic and artistic world, told me, that when in Finland he called with some friends at a roadside cottage, and desired to be accommodated with some boiled eggs, a portion of which were to be boiled hard. The damsel who

---

[45] Merrifield, Ralph. *The Archaeology of Ritual and Magic.* New York: New Amsterdam Books 1987, 143.
[46] Ibid., 167.

superintended the boiling chanted a sing-song charm during the culinary process. This she repeated twice, and turned herself round six times; the soft boiled eggs where then considered to be sufficiently done. She then repeated her verse for a third time, and turned herself round thrice; when the hard boiled eggs were deemed to be ready for eating. They had no clock, dial, clepsydra, hour-glass, burning of tapers, or any other method of measuring time necessary for the egg boiling, than this chanting of the song; and a like kind of formula was repeated for similar domestic purposes, these 'household words' being supposed to depend for their efficacy upon the full belief in the charm they were presumed to cause. The application of this to the incantations of witches over the concoction of some 'hell-broth' is sufficiently obvious. [47]

Many old sayings, such as "God bless you" or simply "bless you" when a person sneezes or "bread and butter" when two people walk around a tree or pole on opposite sides are a continuation of the use of "magical words" and charms. At one time, it was believed that a person who sneezes actually dies during the duration of the sneeze. Another person who uses what was believed to be a magical charm, "God bless you" would ensure that the sneezer's heart would start again. [48]

Likewise, "bread and butter" was a prescribed verbal charm to ensure that arguments would not occur between two persons who happened to walk around an obstruction on

---

[47] Bede, Cuthbert. "Domestic Incantations" in *Notes and Queries*, Vol. 42 S. (86) August 22, 1857, 145.
[48] Roberts, A.H. "We Aren't Magicians, But…Verbal Charms Survive in the Machine Age" in *Tennessee Folklore Society Bulletin, number 18, 1952, 83*

opposite sides. Obviously, these two verbal charms have continued to survive into modern society.

Charms were often used to avoid evil and bad luck. These particular charms were, such as the horseshoe, called "lucky charms." Healing charms have also been extremely popular throughout time. One legend speaks of Christ healing his horse that had suffered a sprain. He reportedly chanted "Bone to bone, sinew to sinew, vein to vein." Recorded in an early German medieval manuscript this same charm was used by Woden to heal the leg of Balder's horse. Obviously, a pagan invocation passed down into Christian folklore.

Magic Wands

Wands are certainly symbolic of the Wiccan practitioner of today but they were also valued tools in ancient society. The followers of Dionysus in ancient Greece used them. Historian J.B. Bury wrote: "The worshippers gathered at night on the mountains, by torchlight, with deer skins on their shoulders and long ivy-wreathed wands in their hands, and danced wildly to the noise of cymbals and flutes." [49]

Likewise, wands or "rods" were utilized in ancient Egypt for protective reasons. In Egypt, three forms of wands existed. The snake-shaped, the apotropaic, or protective wand, and the magic rod.

The snake-shaped wand was normally made of bronze and was either elongated or coiled. Dating back to 2181 BCE, these wands may have represented the goddess Weret Hekau ("Great of Magic"), taking the form of the cobra. If we recall our Biblical mythology, the priests of the Pharaoh used wands

---

[49] Bury, J.B. *A History of Greece to the Death of Alexander the Great.* New York: Modern Library, n.d., 298.

that turned into serpents when Moses first appeared to ask for the release of the Hebrews.

Apotropaic wands were usually made of hippopotamus ivory but could also be constructed of calcite, ebony or faience. According to Oakes and Gahlin, "All manner of weird and wonderful magical imagery decorate these wands, including dancing baboons, snake-breathing lions, winged quadrupeds, human-headed winged snakes," and other fantastical images. [50]

Any inscriptions made on these wands were protective in manner and normally refer to the well-being of women and children.

Finally, we have the "magic wand" which dates back as far as 2055 BCE (of course they probably existed earlier but those found so far date from this period). These "rods" were made from glazed steatite or from such common materials as sticks and branches — or, as Oakes and Gahlin referred to them, the "poor man's bronze or ivory wand". [51]

Magic rods were often decorated with images of frogs, turtles, baboons, crocodiles, lions and leopards, and mystical symbols such as lamps and eyes. The purpose of these wands may have been to dominate the animals represented on them and to use the powers of the animals as protective devices. Additionally, the wands may have been used to command spirits and demons.

The wand, according to Cooper, is "an attribute of all magicians, shamans and medicine men....The Gaelic 'white wand' of power was of yew; the Celtic magic wand was hazel." [52]

---

[50] Oakes and Gahlin, op cit. 453.
[51] Ibid.
[52] Cooper, J.C. *An Illustrated Encyclopaedia of Traditional Symbols*. London: Thames and Hudson Ltd. 1978, 187.

Today the wand is symbolic of the power and authority of the magician and is used to command the forces of magic. The wand is commonly used by the Wiccan practitioner to define the "magic" circle, a protective space where all natural magic is performed, which is regarded was a doorway between worlds and time.

A wand called the "charm wand" manufactured in the 18th and 19 centuries carried on the tradition of the Egyptian wands. Made of glass, these objects were shaped liked rolling pins and contained twisted multicolored beads, threads or seeds. They may have been used to combat the Evil Eye but were also said to have the ability to attract sickness from others thereby protecting the household. These "charm wands" are still occasionally found in antique stores and have become quite collectible.

A modern day wand. This handcrafted wand is made of oak with two crystals at either end to direct power; it is also adorned with protective runes and feathers that symbolize instinctual power and knowledge. This wand is approximately twenty years old. (Author's collection)

II
The Use of Magic in Christianity

The use of magic is not confined to pagan religions, Satanists or New Age followers. Magic has been an accepted part of traditional Christianity since the Christian religion began. However, it is a matter of perspective with Christians viewing the use of magic and spells as works of the Devil rather than as an acceptable religious act, and so the magic and spells used are classified and defined as liturgy and acts of God.

"During the first few centuries of our era," noted George Luck, "Christians were not expressly forbidden to practice magic. Priests provided amulets and charms for the faithful, and a fifth-century Bishop was very familiar with pagan magic." [53] During and after the fifth century the Church did take a more active role to condemn the use of magic and St. Augustine argued that magic could only be performed with the help of demons. In fact, much of the Christian liturgy was used in early "medical" handbooks to cure illness. One such handbook, the Wolfsthurn book, "recommends not only Christian prayers but also apparently meaningless combinations of words or letters for their medical value. At one point, it says to copy out the letters 'P.N.B.C.P.X.A.O.P.I.L,' followed by the Latin for 'in the name of the Father, and the Son, and of the Holy Spirit.' For demonic possession, the book recommends that a priest should speak into the afflicted person's ear the following jumble of Latin, garbled Greek, and gibberish:

---

[53] Luck, George. "Witches and Sorcerers in Classical Literature" in *Witchcraft and Magic in Europe: Ancient Greece and Rome.* Philadelphia: University of Pennsylvania Press 1999, 158.

'Amara Tonta Tyra post hos firabis ficaliri Elypolis starras polyque lique linarras buccabor uel barton vel Titram celi massis Metumbor o priczoni Jordan Ciriacus Valenntinus.'" [54]

A similar handbook called the Munich manual was written in Latin by someone who was probably a member of the Catholic clergy. The book gives instructions on summoning demons with magic circles, commanding spirits and forcing them to return to their hellish homes once they were no longer required. Kiechhefer reports that the author advisers his readers that they will need wax images of people that they wish to afflict along with rings, swords and other ritual items. He also requires, for some spells, a sacrifice be made to the evil spirits and the use of burning herbs to act as magical incense. [55]

As Keith Thomas notes, the Church was rather possessive of those things it considered "legitimate" magic:

"So long as theologians permitted the use of, say, holy water or consecrated bells in order to dispel storms, there was nothing 'superstitious' about such activity; the Church...had no compunction about licensing its own brand of magical remedies." [56]

Today many of these "magical remedies" have survived in the form of prayer, incantation, holy water, sacred incense, bells, set rituals and holy books.

In Christian theology, notes Keith Thomas, the distinction between magic and religion "was an impossibly fine one." [57] In fact it regarded the wearing of amulets and charms as having "no superstition...provided no non-Christian symbols

---

[54] Kieckhefer, Richard. *Magic in the Middle Ages.* Cambridge: Cambridge University Press 1989, 4.
[55] Ibid., 6.
[56] Thomas, Keith. *Religion and the Decline of Magic.* London: Penguin Books 1973, 303.
[57] Ibid., 33.

were also employed." [58] Of course, most amulets were directly tied to pagan origins but this was outside the realm of discussion and still is today.

The various parishes made substantial sums of money during the Middle Ages in creating and selling amulets and charms among other religious relics such as pieces of the True Cross and the head of John the Baptist. It became quite a wonder when John the Baptist's head was exhibited, and sold, in multiple locations around Europe one year.

"While ordinary parish priests may have dabbled in medicine," writes Kieckhefer, "they were more likely to practice other forms of magic." [59]

One form of magic that the priests were called upon to use was for the fertility of fields. Taking a whole day, the priest, before sunrise, would dig four clumps of soil from each of the four sides of the affected field. He would then sprinkle a mixture of holy water, oil, milk and honey on the clumps of earth along with herbs and fragments of trees. He would then recite, in Latin, "Be fruitful and multiply, and fill the earth." Prayers would then be said. After the prayers, the four clumps of earth were taken back to the parish church where four masses were sung over them. Before the sun set the clumps were moved and spread over the field. It was believed that the clumps of earth had fertile power, which would result in a good crop. [60]

The difference between pagan spell-craft and magic and that employed by the Christian Church is simply a matter of terminology. Christian magic is referred to as "ritual power" and acceptable while perhaps identical rituals by other peoples are "witchcraft" and "sorcery."

---

[58] Ibid.
[59] Kieckhefer, op cit., 58.
[60] Ibid.

As the Church struggled to gain a foothold in pagan lands it used what it could to compete with the wise women and cunning men by, according to Harvard anthropologist William Howells, "allowing a certain amount of Christian magic to be used and sanctioned; holy relics, exorcism, and so on." [61]

Ancient Christian spells that have been documented include, among others, healing spells using the Gospel of Matthew; spells invoking Christ for protection against illnesses; protective spells that invoke the sun; spells for healthy childbirth; erotic attraction spells; spells to make a woman pregnant; spells for men to attract a male lover; curses to make a man impotent; spells to obtain a good singing voice; spells to silence a dog, and spells using voodoo dolls. All of these have long been associated with witchcraft; however, they are all Christian spells dating from the first to the 12th century CE. [62]

A bowl, dating to from the early 1st century to late 2nd century CE was discovered by French archaeologists in the waters of the great harbor of Alexandria, Egypt. The bowl was engraved in Latin, "Dia Crstou O Goistais" which has been interpreted to read "by Christ the magician." Long before Jesus was regarded as being the Son of God, his followers believed that he was a great magician. The bowl was most likey used by a "wiseman"or "Magi" in divination rituals.

The Church's implements of worship were viewed as powerful amulets. "Wax blessed on the feast of the Purification," notes Kieckhefer, "was thought effective against thunderbolts. Ringing of church bells could safeguard the

---

[61] Howells, William. *The Heathens: Primitive Man and His Religions.* New York: The Natural History Library/Anchor Books 1962, 105

[62] Meyer, Marvin W. and Richard Smith, ed. *Ancient Christian Magic.* Princeton: Princeton University Press 1994.

parish from storms. ...Long sheets of parchment or paper, inscribed with prayers and then rolled up, could protect their bearers against sudden death, wounding by weapons, the slander of false witnesses, evil spirits, tribulations, illness, danger in childbirth, and other afflictions." [63]

The spells used by Coptic Christians, according to David Frankfurter, "demonstrate that the lines between 'magic,' medicine, and religion that are customarily assumed in modern conversation simply did not exist" [64] to the practitioners during that time.

For the Christian magician and his client it was important to incorporate as much of the official Church liturgy as possible "by ritually appealing to powers that are acknowledged and venerated by the temple or the church, often doing so with the very gestures, articles, and language..." [65]

The use of magic and spells in Christianity increased during the Renaissance when "magic was used as a means to bring higher angelic forces down to the ordinary world." [66]

Magic has always been an integral part of Christianity and continues today in Catholicism. Protestant sects, however, have always rallied against magic and this attitude is one of the basic tenets of the Protestant faith, which resulted in the Reformation and the attempted destruction of Catholicism. Under Protestant rule, during the Reformation, Christians were forbidden to undertake such "magical" practices as "...casting holy water upon his bed...bearing about him holy bread, or St. John's Gospel...ringing of holy bells; or blessing

---

[63] Kieckhefer, op cit. 78.
[64] Frankfurter, David. "Healing Spells" in Meyer, Marvin W. and Richard Smith, ed. *Ancient Christian Magic*. Princeton: Princeton University Press 1994, 79.
[65] Ibid., 80.
[66] Greenwood, Susan. *The Encyclopedia of Magic & Witchcraft*. London: Hermes House 2005, 28.

with the holy candle, to the intent thereby to be discharged of the burden of sin, or to drive away dreams and fantasies; or…putting trust and confidence of health and salvation in the same ceremonies." [67]

It is ironic that the Protestants viewed the Catholic Church as Satanic when the Catholic Church was responsible for the witch trials in the first place. A 16th century woodcut of a Protestant caricature of Pope Alexander VI (below) shows him as a demon. It is interesting to note, however, that the Catholic nations had a much less intense witch-hunt than Protestant nations. Some scholars have suggested that the belief in witchcraft and the resulting slaughter were due to the Reformation and the religious struggle that it caused. The Protestant focus was not so much the removal of evil and witchcraft but the removal of all "pagan" influences and the spirituality that paganism represented.

---

[67] Ibid., 140.

The History & Use of Amulets, Charms and Talismans

"The Papist Devil" From a Reformation handbill against Pope Alexander VI, Paris, 15th century. "Ego sum Papa"=I am the Pope.

Gary R. Varner

III
Amulets in Witchcraft and Sorcery

While witchcraft has existed throughout history, unexplained illnesses did not always result in diagnoses that indicated that witchcraft or sorcery was the cause. Thomsen noted, "In more than half of the cases a god was thought responsible for the illness; ghosts account for about a fifth, and various demons for most of the rest. Witchcraft, however, is mentioned in less than 5 percent of the instances, although there are a lot of incantations, rituals and medical texts to avert evil." [68]

Evil itself was the major fear of people—not necessarily the witch, and evil was everywhere. Amulets of every kind were utilized to avert evil, including such simple things as wearing a string of wool, carrying a stone, which had a natural hole worn in it, or a ring made of a particular metal or stone.

It is interesting that some amulets were carvings or images of demons, which were worn to counteract evil from other quarters. These amulets were normally worn on necklaces and were inscribed with various incantations. Tablets with incantations were often hung up in homes—these too are amulets. The reasons for hanging these items in the home are the same as the hanging of crucifixes in Christian homes—protection from evil by representations of deity.

---

[68] Thomsen, Marie-Louise. "Witchcraft and Magic in Ancient Mesopotamia," in *Witchcraft and Magic in Europe: Biblical and Pagan Societies,* edited by Bengt Ankarloo and Stuart Clark. Philadelphia: University of Pennsylvania Press 2001, 32.

Words are perhaps the most potent form of the amulet. Incantations, metrical and nonsensical words and sounds as well as written spells or "charms" were very common in the past.

Written symbols, cryptograms, magic squares and other combinations, as described previously, were, according to Merrifield, "not only used for malevolent magic but could serve as a protective amulet also." [69] The very act of writing and the ability to use the written word took on a metaphysical quality all of its own. Written charms became the "stock-in-trade of countless magicians, 'wise men and women', 'white witches and wizards' and other wonder-workers," Merrifield wrote, "whose craft survived in some rural parts of Britain into the present century." [70] During the Roman period in England many of these written charms were made of rolled up lead tablets.

We know from the number of these lead "curse tablets" found in the ancient world, from the Mediterranean countries to Roman occupied Britain, that most everyone at one time or another practiced spell-craft—and not always for benevolent purposes.

More than 1600 curse tablets have been discovered so far and the majority are written in Greek. At least 130 have been found at the Roman spa known as Bath in England. Researchers suspect that close to 500 additional tablets may still be uncovered at Bath. Those that are not written in Greek are in Latin and have been found in the Western regions of the Roman Empire.

The oldest tablets date to at least the 5th century BCE and were concerned with business curses, theatrical competitions,

---

[69] Merrifield, Ralph. *The Archeology of Ritual and Magic.* New York: New Amsterdam Books 1987, 142.
[70] Ibid.

or erotic-attraction spells. From the 4th century BCE to the 4th century, CE the focus was on erotic-attraction or those having to do with athletic contests.[71]

Luck reports that many curse tablets appear to have been written by the same person signifying that a professional sorcerer was producing such tablets. "Some of these professionals," he wrote, "probably worked for lawyers whose clients were desperate to win their cases."[72] Many people today would agree that lawyers have a similar relationship with such sorcerers.

Ogden reports that the most important aspect of the curse tablet was its deposition. "There were five major contexts for this," he writes "in a grave, in a chthonic sanctuary, in a body of water, in a place of specific relevance to the curse or its victim, or in a non-chthonic sanctuary. A recipe for the manufacture of a curse tablet recommends that it be deposited in 'river, land, sea, stream coffin or well.'" [73]

"A variation of the idea of depositing curse tablets in graves," noted Ogden, "was to deposit them on a battlefield or in a place of execution. The 200 or so fragments of tablets from Amathous in Cyprus were deposited in a particularly appropriate site…They were found at the bottom of a shaft under a mass of human bones." [74]

Treated like legal documents and compacts between the solicitor and the Gods, the tablets were tossed into the water to obtain justice and love, ensure winnings at the racetrack,

---

[71] Ogden, Daniel. "Binding Spells: Curse Tablets and Voodoo Dolls in the Greek and Roman Worlds" in *Witchcraft and Magic in Europe; Ancient Greece and Rome*. Philadelphia: University of Pennsylvania Press 1999, 4.
[72] Luck, George. "Witches and Sorcerers in Classical Literature" in *Witchcraft and Magic in Europe: Ancient Greece and Rome*. Philadelphia: University of Pennsylvania Press 1999, 108.
[73] Ogden, op cit.15.
[74] Ibid., 17.

and to request retribution for perceived wrongs. Curse tablets and binding spells were so common in antiquity that even Plato, in his *Republic*, remarked how cheaply they could be obtained. While not all curse tablets were left at wells or springs, during the imperial period at least, water became the preferred place of deposition. Wells, springs and other underground water sources were believed to have "sympathetic significance" and the cold water was an easy way to "set", or "bind", the tablet and the victim. It has been noted by researchers that one of the tablets from Bath "prays that its victims should become as liquid as water". [75]

While there were certain "recipes" for the completion of a curse tablet and many had exotic additions of Egyptian or Jewish influence, there was no specific "witch" responsible for them nor were the creators in any way tied to any formal witchcraft. However, the traditions at the time allowed for these formalized curses to be created by the general populace to resolve various personal issues.

Ogden points out that curse tablets were not considered unusual and in reality were part of the "ordinary religious practice in the 'prayers for justice' category,' in which tablets can be phrased as quite normal prayers to mainline deities." [76] While this practice may seem to embrace witchcraft today, in the ancient world "any curse tablet that appeals to a mainline deity, directly or indirectly, cannot be excluded from the sphere of 'religion.'" [77]

A curse tablet was discovered during the 2005-2006 excavation in Leicester, England (photo on next page). Archaeologists from the University of Leicester, during an excavation in the Vine Street area in the city's historic core,

---

[75] Ibid., 23.
[76] Ogden op cit., 85.
[77] Ibid.

found a lead curse tablet dating to the second or third century CE.

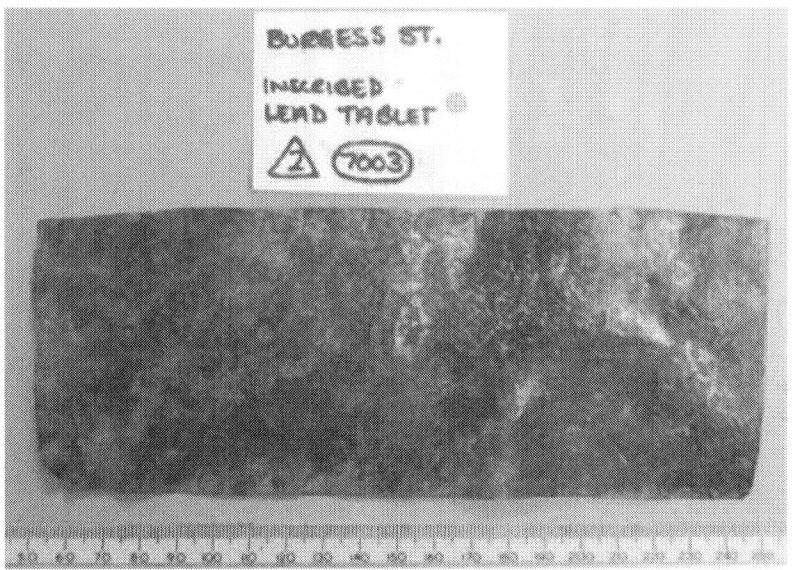

Leicester Lead Curse Tablet (Photo courtesy University of Leicester)

The handwritten Latin script has been translated to read as follows:

"To the god Maglus, [78] I give the wrongdoer who stole the cloak of Servandus. Silvester, Riomandus (etc.)…that he destroy him before the ninth day, the person who stole the cloak of Servandus…"[79] The tablet then lists 19 possible suspects. According to Richard Buckley, co-director of the University's Archaeological Services, "most curses seem to relate to thefts and typically the chosen god is asked to do harm to the perpetrator. It has been suggested, on the basis of name forms and the value of items stolen, that the curses

---

[78] "Maglus" is believed to be a title such as "prince" in Gaelic.
[79] "University of Leicester archaeologists unearth ancient curse." Press release from University of Leicester, November 30, 2006.

relate to the lives of ordinary people, rather than the wealthy, and that they were perhaps commissioned by the dedicator from a professional writer." [80]

More recently, a lead tablet written in Greek was discovered at the old city kingdom of Amathus on the island of Cyprus. Part of the text reads: "May your penis hurt when you make love." Dating to the 7th century CE, long after Christianity had been established on Cyprus, archaeologists believe that it was a survival of pagan shamanism or witchcraft. [81]

Graf notes that the texts written on the lead or papyri "are prayers, ritualistic utterances to which writing gives unalterable permanence. At the same time that the spell was engraved on lead, it was spoken." [82] The vocalization was performed as an act to "accompany and describe the ritual action." [83]

Water acts as an energy source, to "electrify" objects, and plays an important part in both magic and religion. Water is a conductor of information, including spells and curses. One curse found in a well in Attic was addressed: "I am sending this letter to Hermes and Persephone…". [84] The sender was relying on the water's ability to transport the request to the underworld.

Curses were commonly inscribed on papyrus, paper, wax or lead tablets and slate. "Cursing wells" were not uncommon

---

[80] Ibid.
[81] "Sex Curse found at ancient Cyprus site: report" Agence France-Presse, http://afp.google.com/article/ALeqM5gs7KYHLwaf0TeF4bnNkYp1xS6ZvQ, 7/12/2008.
[82] Graf, Fritz. *Magic in the Ancient World.* trans. by Franklin Philip. Cambridge: Harvard University Press 1997, 207.
[83] Ibid.
[84] Graf, op cit, 131.

in Wales. To be effective, the well had to have a northern exposure.

Merrifield reports that, at least in Anglesey, Wales, "slate seems to have been considered a specially appropriate material for cursing...Perhaps because of its leaden colour." [85]

A specific ritual was also required to place curses at the Anglesey "cursing well":

Martin Shore, senior site supervisor, with the curse tablet he excavated at Leicester. (Photo courtesy University of Leicester)

"A slate with the name of the person to be cursed scratched upon it, or a wretched frog pierced with pins, was thrown into the well by the curser, who then crawled round the well against the path of the sun, uttering appropriate

---

[85] Merrifield, op cit. 155.

curses. This was called 'well-wishing', signifying the exact opposite of the ordinary meaning of that term." [86]

Rhys wrote about this Welsh cursing well, called Ffynnon Elian, in his book *Celtic Folklore Welsh and Manx*:

> (The priestess of the well) "kept a book in which she registered the name of each evil wisher for a trifling sum of money. When this had been done, a pin was dropped into the well in the name of the victim. …the trade in curses seems to have been a very thriving one: its influence was powerful and widespread." [87]

Those who had been named as victims could also pay a small sum and have their names removed from the book.

In ancient Greece, even the State instituted formal curses to defend itself. One was all-inclusive, defending Greece from harmful spells or poisons, obstruction of the transportation of corn in Greek territory, rebellion, and the betrayal of public officials. The curse, inscribed in stone, read, "If anyone in office does not perform this curse at the statue of Dynamis when the games are convened at the Anthesteria or the festival of Heracles or that of Zeus, he is to be the object of the curse." In addition, it cautions, "If anyone breaks the inscription on which this curse has been written, or chips off the letters, or rubs them smooth, he is to die, himself and his family with him." [88]

Similar devices to avoid evil spirits and witchcraft continue to be used into contemporary times around the world. The photograph on page 44 is that of a "nail figure," *Nkisi Nkondi*, from the Congo. Carved between 1880 and 1920, this voodoo doll-type wooden figure, or "fetish", was used by

---

[86] Ibid.
[87] Rhys, John. *Celtic Folklore: Welsh and Manx*. New York: Gordon Press 1973, 397.
[88] Ogden, Daniel. *Magic, Witchcraft, and Ghosts in the Greek and Roman Worlds*. Oxford: Oxford University Press 2002, 275-276.

families and whole communities to prevent illness, weaken evil spirits, and repel evil deeds. The shaman would "activate" this powerful and protective figure by exploding gunpowder in front of it or driving nails into it. Since the figure was often used to seal agreements between people, the phase "to hammer out a deal" resulted from the act of driving nails into it at the end of the bargaining session.

These nail figures were used to identify and hunt down unknown wrongdoers such as thieves, and people who were believed to cause sickness through witchcraft. They were also used to punish people who swore false oaths and villages which broke treaties.

While the Nikisi Nkondi was a "white magic" object it was no less a tool of witchcraft. Hostile to outsiders, the figure was imbued with magical powers by the shaman who placed special herbs and medicines in the chest cavity. Nails were usually personalized in some way before they were driven in - for example, by being kissed or licked or having hair or other distinctive materials tied to them. Should the user break the oath, the spirit in the image would know from the saliva or other bodily traces on the nail whom to annihilate or punish. The many nails covering the torso of this figure attest to the large number of individuals who sought its powers.

In tribal society, amulets and charms are very important and worn by anyone concerned with safety and survival. Many times these amulets turn up in relatively unexpected places.

In Africa, knives and daggers continue to be important pieces of any man's wardrobe. Many of these weapons have carvings of symbols made into the blade or handles that have supernatural meaning. The photograph below shows one such example from the Sudan. The "S" carving on the blade is believed to represent a wicked double bladed hand weapon intended to combat any evil spirit or force that may attempt to endanger the wearer. This double bladed weapon is a ritual knife still reportedly used in Syria in the 20th century. Because the markings represent significant material objects this particular dagger may have been a status symbol as well. The owner most likely was an important man in the tribal structure.

Nkisi Nkondi, or "nail figure" from the Congo. Photograph by the author and courtesy Carnegie Museum of Natural History, Pittsburgh, Pennsylvania.

Sudanese dagger.

Other symbols incorporated into weapons include those in the Ngbondi spear from the Congo. The design, which appears to represent a solar/planetary symbol has an unknown meaning but is present on all Ngbondi spears and may be of some magical purpose. This example is probably well over 100 years in age. According to researchers, the Ngbondi spear was also used as a way to purchase items of need. Five such spears could buy a slave while it took 50 to purchase a wife.

The History & Use of Amulets, Charms and Talismans

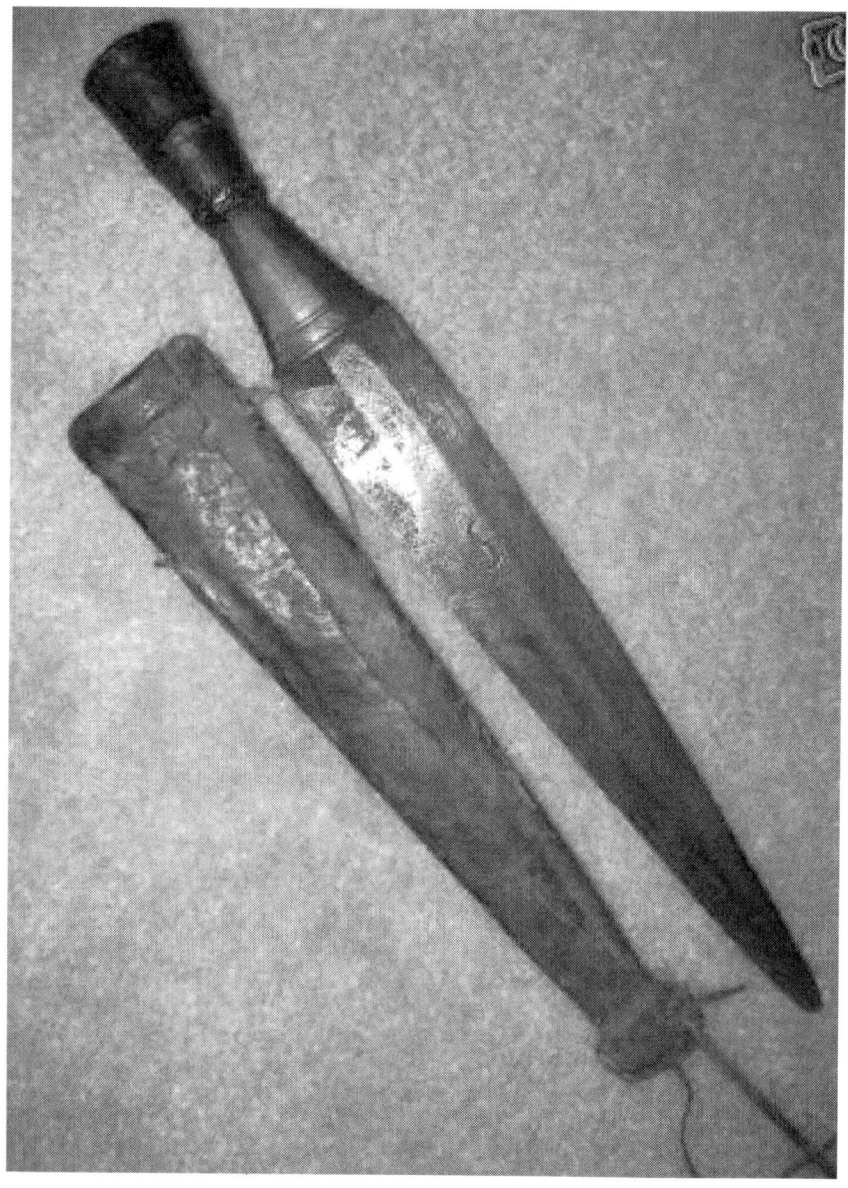

Ngbondi spear shaft.

Engraved blades are commonly found on ethnic weapons such as the Sudanese knife shown on the following page. The blade has been etched in colored designs of an apparent solar representation. The true meanings are, again, unknown but probably served more than a pleasing artistic rendering of an abstract idea. Some have theorized that many of these designs have been taken from ancient rock art, which is then duplicated as adopted symbolism for animal brands and other purposes.

Swords have been used as protective and healing instruments as well in some parts of the world. Among German and East European Jews, a bronze or steel sword was suspended over the head of women in childbirth to ensure a successful birth. In China swords are hung above the bed to protect against evil.

War amulets such as these were made to protect the owner from being wounded or killed, to give him strength and courage and to invoke the gods in his favor.

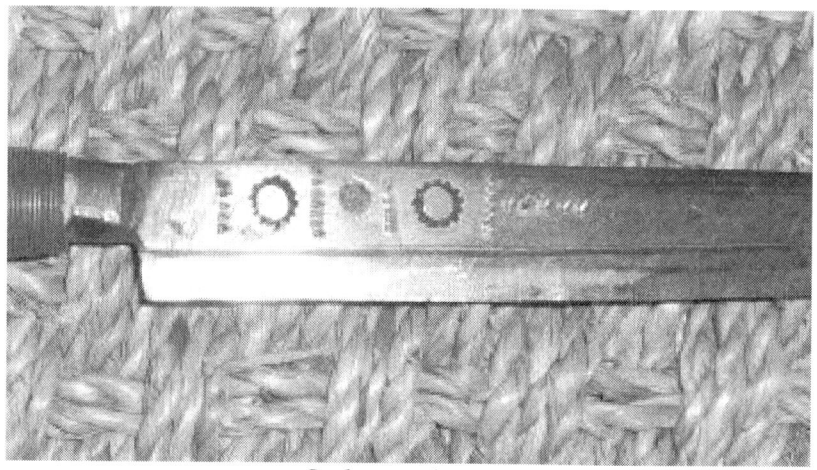

Sudanese dagger.

The Indonesian *kris* is a magical implement itself and each blade is said to be inhabited by a spirit which often moves on its own volition.

Kris blades are still commonly used and made in Malaysia and Indonesia. Each kris is considered a living thing with its own soul, capable of bringing either good or bad luck. They were also thought to have the capability to act on their own, jumping out of their scabbards to engage a perceived enemy.

The kris, originating in the 14th century, is always formed of three layers of steel or iron with thinner layers fitted between and then twisted or beaten into shape. Most often, the kris was decorated with engravings of demons or dragons.

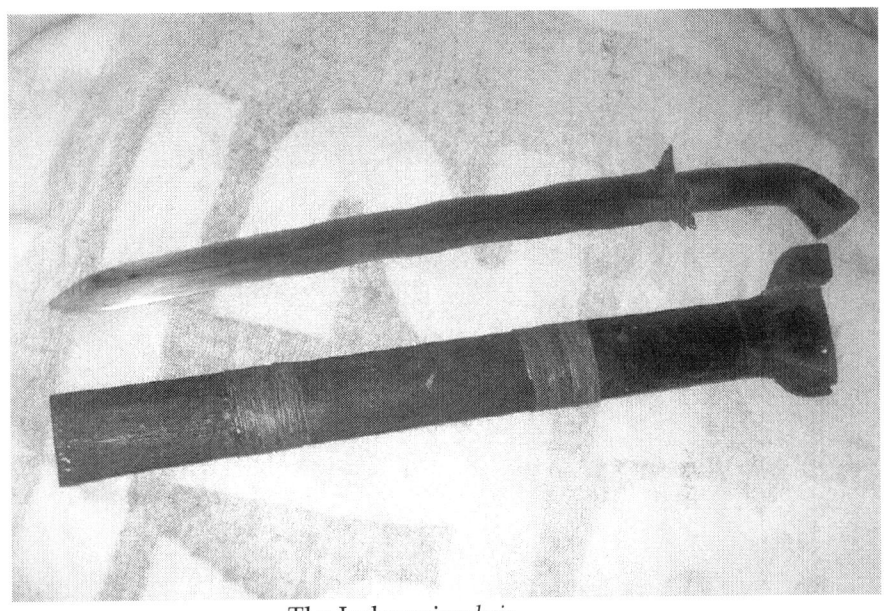

The Indonesian *kris*.

The kris was intended for three purposes:
1. A thrusting weapon
2. A religious cult object, and
3. An executioner's weapon.

However, it also became an item of apparel and most every Indonesian/Malayan male would wear on at his side.

According to martial arts expert, Ramon Villardo [89] the kris "is regarded as man's tutelary spirit and a means of communicating with one's ancestors."

Some of the mythology and folklore associated with the kris indicates that people have said that they have seen water drawn from the blade—more than likely due to the curved or "wavy" nature of the blade itself. Villard also writes "The

---

[89]Villardo, Ramon. "Kris daggers and swords of Indonesia and the Philippines." http://www.bakbakan.com/kris.htm. 3/7/07

very act of death could be performed by merely pointing the weapon at the intended victim…It is also believed to be able to rattle its own scabbard to call notice and warn its owner of an impending danger…" [90]

While others have said the kris is capable of bringing either good or bad, Villardo states "It is a firm belief that the powers of religion and of the kris could only be manifested for good purposes."

However, anecdotal information would appear to present a different picture. Some have been linked to a series of violent deaths, failed businesses and the ability to grant prophetic powers. Extreme care is warranted for those possessing the kris and unusual preservation measures have been taken by some to ensure that the knife remains docile and protected.

Additional anecdotal information is that the kris will move on its own from place to place in the house — it is a truly living being to those familiar with the weapon.

Swords have been the subject of myth for centuries, mostly because of its manufacture. Iron especially is effective against evil spirits, demons, trolls, witches and fairies.

---

[90] Ibid.

IV
Animal Totems

Totem animals are have been an important part of indigenous religions and traditions for thousands of years. Certain animals become linked to tribal groups and clans and are regarded as protectors, as divine mediators and as ancestors. In many cultures, illnesses are believed to be caused by an injury or insult to a totemic animal. Among the Balakai, in Western Equatorial Africa, abnormal births are believed to be caused when their women give birth to a totem animal or animals. The Dinka people of the Upper Nile believe that twins are the result of a woman giving birth to a totem animal and to a human ancestor at the same time.

Totem animals can be any form with cats, frogs and large and dangerous game animals being the most favored. Perhaps the bear is the most ancient of the sacred animals. Cave paintings dating to 32,000-75,000 BP[91] in France and discovery of the intentional arrangement of bear skulls on rock altars, also in caves, indicates that the bear cult was active at least 32 millennia ago in Europe. The bear cult has continued as an important part of the indigenous Ainu culture in Japan. The Ainu, direct decendents of the ancient Jomōn culture, are possibly related to the Tlingit Indians of Alaska who are well known for their artistic renderings of the bear in their tribal art. The bear in Ainu belief is the god of the mountain, a sacred messenger and culture hero. During one of the Ainu ceremonies, called the *iyomante,* a bear is ritually slain so that its soul is sent back to the land of the gods. There are many legends among indigenous people around the

---

[91] BP=Before Present

world that tell of a human woman mating with a bear and producing offspring. The Ainu have a similar story. Sir James Frazer wrote, "they have a legend of a woman who had a son by a bear; and many of them who dwell in the mountains pride themselves on being descended from a bear. Such people are called 'Descendents of the bear'…, and in the pride of their heart they will say, 'As for me, I am a child of the god of the mountains…'" [92]

The bear as a sacrificial animal is not only important to the Ainu but to the Delaware Indians living in Ontario, Canada. During the Big House ceremony, which is held at Hagersville, Ontario on the first full moon in January, a hibernating bear is driven from its den, brought to the Big House and killed with a blow to the head. The bear is eaten in a ceremonial meal and its spirit "rises to Patamawas ('to whom prayers are offered'), bearing with it the prayers of mankind."[93] The bear is viewed as a lunar power around the world and the astronomical signs of the Big House ceremony indicate this is true to North American Indians as well.

The bear is associated with resurrection (due to its hibernating ability), and thus with rebirth and renewal. It also is known for its supernatural powers, strength, bravery and stamina. It was sacred to Artemis and Diana—both goddesses of nature. Young Greek girls used to dance to Artemis in the guise of bears, wearing both bear masks and bear costumes and were called "Arktoi", meaning "she-bears". [94] Norse warriors also dressed in bear skins for battle and were so

---

[92] Frazer, Sir James. *The Golden Bough: A study in magic and religion.* Hertfordshire: Wordsworth Editions 1993, 505-506.
[93] Krickeberg, Walter & et al. *Pre-Columbian American Religions.* New York: Holt, Rinehart and Winston 1968, 166.
[94] Baring, Anne and Jules Cashford. *The Myth of the Goddess: Evolution of an Image.* London: Arkana/Penguin Books 1991, 326.

fierce and impervious to sword and fire that they became known as "berserkers."

In Mongolian shamanism, the bear is regarded as lord of the animals and is revered as an ancestor. The bear is called *baabgai,* which means "father". Stewart tells us that the Mongolians regard the literal name for the bear as taboo, "given that the bear is recognized as an ancestor by almost all Siberian peoples". [95] While the bear is hunted at times, it is treated with great respect and the skulls are placed on poles or in trees or placed on a platform as shamans are after death. Like the dog in other cultures, the bear is believed by some Siberian people to oversee the journey of the soul to the underworld.

The bear is a messenger of forest spirits in shamanism and this concept carried over to the Slavic traditions. The *Leshii*, that Faery-like shape-changer who was master of the forest and protector of animals, used both the wolf and the bear as special servants. The bear would not only serve the Leshii but protect him.

Inuit and Lapp shamans will shape-shift into bear form for their spirit journeys.

Like the Mongolians, the use of the "regular" name for the bear in Apache culture was also prohibited. According to ethnologist Morris Edward Opler, "...the Chiricahua would seldom say the regular word for bear. They would call it 'mother's sibling.' It doesn't like to be called by the regular word. It gets after you when you say that." [96] In other words, the bear will cause illness if it is addressed directly with its regular name. The Apache did not hunt, eat or use the skins of

---

[95] Sarangerel (Julie Ann Stewart). *Riding Windhorses: A Journey into the Heart of Mongolian Shamanism.* Rochester: Destiny Books 2000, 33.
[96] Opler, Morris Edward. *An Apache Life-Way: The Economic, Social, and Religious Institutions of the Chiricahua Indians.* Chicago: The University of Chicago Press 1941, 224.

bear and avoided it as much as possible. According to one of Opler's informants, "If you come in contact with the track of a bear, or a tree where the bear has leaned, or bear manure, or if you sleep where a bear has sat down, or if you come in contact with a bear by smell or touch, you can get sick." [97]

The reason for the avoidance of the word "bear", no matter the language, was, as E.P. Evans noted, because the bear was "looked upon, not merely as rapacious brutes, whose physical strength and voracity were to be feared, but rather as incarnations of mysterious and malignant forces capable of inflicting injuries by occult and magical influences, and therefore not to be enraged or irritated in any manner. For this reason," Evans continues, "they were not called by their real names, but were propitiated by flattering epithets..." [98]

Like many other sacred icons of other more ancient religions, the bear, in Christian theology, represented the Devil, evil, cruelty and carnal appetite. Evans describes one relief on the door of a cathedral in Hildesheim, carved in 1015, "which depicts a bear stand(ing) behind Pilate, whispering into his ear and filing his mind with diabolical suggestions". [99]

While it may seem incongruous that the bear, known for its size and savagery, has been worshipped for its Mother Goddess aspects it is the loving relationship that the adult bear has with its young that denotes this special association. Tamra Andrews noted "Bears were almost always connected in some way to the female life force, either being female themselves and giving birth or being the offspring of a human

---

[97] Ibid. 225.
[98] Evans, E.P. *Animal Symbolism in Ecclesiastical Architecture.* London: W. Heineman 1896, 8
[99] Ibid, 88

female. This quality reinforced the bears' intimate connection with fertility, renewal, and, often, the moon." [100]

The goddess Artio ("bear goddess"), worshipped in the Berne (Celtic for "bear") area of Switzerland during the 4th century CE, was the protectress of bears against hunters. She also protected humans from the wrath of the bear! Artio was a goddess of plenty, which ties into the bear's associations with fertility and renewal. Bear amulets have been found in North Britain and other areas and have been found in burials. A small child was found buried near Malton in Yorkshire with a tiny black bear-amulet [101] showing perhaps the belief that the bear helped the soul on its way to the underworld.

Aside from the Apache, the bear was an important spiritual totem to many Native American people. The bear is associated with sacred and powerful water sites and was regarded as a major deity and source of power. Bear doctors could shape-shift from human to bear by swimming in a special pool. Once in the water the doctor would emerge in a bear form and could only change back into his human form by submerging once again in the same pool. The bear has many of the characteristics of water. It is symbolic of rebirth and renewal; it is connected to the feminine life force and fertility. The bear was thought to be the creator of geysers in California; the spirit of the bear was believed to heat the water for curative purposes, which were utilized extensively by the local tribes.

In Lakota belief, the bear "is the friend of the Great Spirit. He is very wise."[102] The bear instructed the shaman in ceremonial secrets, song and medicines. To the Lakota, if a

---

[100] Andrews, Tamra. *A Dictionary of Nature Myths*. Oxford: Oxford University Press 1998, 25.
[101] Green, Miranda. *The Gods of the Celts*. Glouchester: Alan Sutton 1986, 184.
[102] Walker, James R. *Lakota Belief and Ritual*. Lincoln: University of Nebraska Press 1991, 116.

man sees a bear in his dreams or visions he must become a medicine man. The Lakota believe that the bear is the only creature that knows all things about the Great Spirit and is totally conversant in the language of the shaman. The bear is referred to as "the God the Bear," and presides over "love and hate and bravery and wounds and many kinds of medicines." He was also "the patron of mischief and fun." [103]

"The Bears" is one of the Oglala Sioux sodalities, a "dream cult" made up of individuals who have had the same vision. Called the *Mato ihanblapi* ("they dream of bears") the members would dress for their ceremonies as bears, parade around the camp, growling like bears while they chased people. According to Powers, these "bear dreamers" were "astute curers". [104]

At one California Miwok site, a large standing stone called the "Northstar stone" was used for ceremonial purposes. It stands with several mortars (areas used for the grinding of food and other materials) on one side, two on the top, and with several incised lines that run the length of one side. It is believed that this stone was a central piece used during bear ceremonies thanking the Grizzly Bear and to welcome the change of season from winter to spring. The mortars were used to grind berries and other food items with the juices running down the incised lines into a catchment at the bottom. It is assumed that the Grizzly was lured into the area and would eat from the catchment, performing its part in the ritual. A bear "footprint" was carved into one portion of the Northstar stone representative of a bear walking in a docile manner, the back print overlapping with the print of the forepaw. The footprint and incised grooves on Northstar are

---

[103] Ibid, 121.
[104] Powers, William K. *Oglala Religion.* Lincoln: University of Nebraska Press 1982, 58.

similar to other "rain rocks" found in Northern California. A similar bear footprint carving is located in Northwestern California and a large carving representing the claw marks of a bear can be seen at Chaw'se, Indian Grinding Rock State Park near Fiddletown, California.

The importance of the bear in Native American culture and religion cannot be minimized. During an archaeological excavation in 1966 in the Sacramento delta area east of Oakley, California, a Plains Miwok burial of a small, five-year old Indian girl was uncovered. The unusual aspect of this burial was that the child was buried with a Grizzly Bear cub of approximately the same size. It appeared to the excavators that the bear cub was slain deliberately to accompany the child to the afterlife. According to the excavation report, the bear was positioned directly behind and to the side of the child with one paw draped over the child's body. [105] To the Plains Indians the bear is believed to be the ruler of underworld creatures so its association with death and the underworld may have been instrumental for its inclusion in the child's burial.

The Athapaskan Indians of British Columbia believe the bear to be the guardian of fire; however, it is the "Bear Mother" that remains the most endearing characterization of this animal. Christopher Manes wrote in *Other Creations: Rediscovering the Spirituality of Animals*, that the Bear Mother is representative of the Mother Goddess. According to Manes:

"Invariably, the feminine animal spirit represents a force for good, even cultural heroism. In the Bear Mother stories....a woman is kidnapped by a bear in the form of a man, who

---

[105] Cowan, R.A., Clewlow, C.W. Jr & et al. "An Unusual Burial of a Bear and Child From the Sacramento Delta", in Institute of Archaeology, University of California Los Angeles Journal of New World Archaeology, Vol 1, Number 2, December 1975, 25-30.

takes her to his village to be his bride. In her new life among the bears, the woman learns their 'songs,' at the same time teaching the bear spirits about human society. The woman usually gives birth to several children by her bear husband who grow up to become leaders or warriors." [106]

1930s building façade with the Bear Mother.

Cats represent clairvoyance, watchfulness, mystery, female malice and sensual beauty. In India, it was believed that cats could take over the bodies of women at will. [107] On the other hand, the Indian goddess of maternity and

---

[106] Manes, Christopher. *Other Creations: Rediscovering the Spirituality of Animals.* New York: Doubleday 1997, 162-163.
[107] Tresidder, Jack. *Symbols and Their Meanings.* London: Duncan Baird Publishers 2000, 59.

protectress of children, Sasti, is a feline goddess that rides on a cat. [108]

The Egyptian cat-goddess Bast

Both Chinese and Japanese folklore view the cat as symbolic of transformation. Scandinavian mythology says that the goddess Freyja's chariot is drawn by cats. In Egyptian mythology the goddess Bast, the moon goddess, is cat-headed and the cat also symbolized the protective aspects of the Mother Goddess, Isis.

In Cambodia, the cat is associated with drought and is carried in cages to rain ravaged areas where it is doused with

---

[108] Mackenzie, Donald A. *Myths and Legends: India.* London: Studio Editions 1985, 153.

water. It is believed that the cat's howls will awaken the rain goddess Indra so that she will stop the downpour. [109]

Big cats have dominated the ancient religious traditions of Mesoamerica. Appearing as a jaguar or puma or as a composite jaguar human figure, the cat gods were associated with caves, the night and the underworld, much as cats were during the witch-hunting days of Europe.

One of the main deities of the Olmec people was the were-jaguar, a half human and half jaguar being. The were-jaguar was important for its rain making abilities. The Maya had the most jaguar deities than any Mesoamerican people. They regarded the jaguar as representative of the sun. Miller and Taube noted that the Mayan jaguar was the nighttime sun, and as god of the Underworld, it was also the Underworld's sun. [110] The jaguar image is frequently associated with sacrifice.

Black cats are normally thought to bring bad luck—except in England where they have the opposite effect. Images of black cats in England are made into good luck charms. Symbologist J. C. Cooper, however, noted, "As black it is lunar, evil and death; it is only in modern times that a black cat has been taken to signify good luck." [111] Ancient Chinese tradition speaks of the black cat as representative of misfortune and, of course, Christian symbolism links the black cat with Satan, lust, laziness and witchcraft.

While cats have caused some fear among humans for their mystical character, it is the cat that has paid the price more often than their human companions have. According to an entry in the January 11, 1851 *Notes and Queries* British

---

[109] Keister, Douglas. *Stories in Stone.* New York: MJF Books 2004, 71.

[110] Miller, Mary and Karl Taube. *The Gods and Symbols of Ancient Mexico and the Maya.* London: Thames and Hudson 1993, 104.

[111] Cooper, J.C. *An Illustrated Encyclopaedia of Traditional Symbols.* London: Thames and Hudson 1978. 30

periodical, "In Wilts, and also in Devon, it is believed that cats born in the Month of May will catch no mice nor rats, but will, contrary to the wont of other cats, bring in snakes and slow worms. Such cats are called 'May cats,' and are held in contempt." [112] "May cats" seem to have been universally disliked in England in the 19th century. Another *Notes and Queries* entry on February 1, 1851 stated "In Hampshire, to this day, we always kill may cats," and in June another reader wrote "…may Cats are unlucky, and will suck the breath of children." [113] This last superstition is still commonly found in the Western world.

Cats are also invariably linked to the weather — and generally not good weather. The approach of wind and rain was said to be foretold by the way a cat washes itself or in what direction it sits while grooming. Greek folklore from the 1890s said "…if a cat licks herself with her face turned towards the north, the wind will soon blow from that dangerous quarter." [114] Witch-lore says that the cat familiar is a rain-maker as well as a companion to the witch. Foretelling the weather by watching a cat may not be foolproof however. Another bit of weather-lore says "Cats with their tails up and hair apparently electrified indicate approaching wind, --or a dog." [115]

Witches have long been associated with the cat — the cat being either an animal familiar or a form that the witch easily transforms into. This relationship is an ancient one; the Greeks and Romans told of a woman who had been changed into a cat chosen as the priestess of Hecate, goddess of the Underworld, sorcery and magic. In fact, Hecate is often

---

[112] *Notes and Queries*, Vol. 3, Number 63, January 11, 1851, 20.
[113] *Notes and Queries*, Vol. 3, Number 87, June 28, 1851, 516.
[114] Inwards, Richard. *Weather Lore.* London: Elliot Stock 1893, 126.
[115] Ibid.

depicted as a cat. It is interesting that the cat is so universally thought of in this manner as, in reality, there are more stories of rabbits being associated with witches than cats. While there is some court testimony in the 16th century concerning witches shape-shifting into cats, many other animals were also implicated such as dogs, frogs, cocks and hares. In 1587 twenty-four Aberdeen witches were tried and eventually "They accused one another of unnatural practices, from eating mutton on Good Friday to concourse with devils in the shape of black cats and dogs." [116]

This belief in witches assuming the form of cats was not restricted to Europe by any means. Folklorist Vance Randolph wrote in his 1947 study, *Ozark Superstitions* that "A witch can assume the form of any bird or animal, but cats and wolves seem to be her favorite disguises. In many a backwoods village you may hear some gossip about a woman who visits her lover in the guise of a house cat. Once inside his cabin, she assumes her natural form and spends the night with him. Shortly before daybreak she becomes a cat again, returns to her home, and is transformed into a woman at her husband's beside." [117]

In popular folklore, the witch was said to be able to assume the form of a black cat nine times — to match the nine magical lives that the cat is supposedly blessed with. Across Medieval Europe, black cats were hunted down and killed — usually by burning. This most often occurred on Shrove Tuesday [118] and Easter.

---

[116] Parrinder, Geoffry. "The Witch as Victim" in *The Witch in History* edited by Venetia Newall. New York: Barnes & Noble 1996, 129.

[117] Randolph, Vance. *Ozark Magic and Folklore.* New York: Dover Publications, Inc. 1964, 268. A reprint of *Ozark Superstitions* published 1947 by Columbia University Press.

[118] Shrove Tuesday is the last day before Lent. It was a day that became popular for divination among many other activities.

In fact, notes Thompson, "the connection of the cat with witches was no doubt the reason for the persecution and ill-treatment of the animal in the seventeenth century." [119]

Cats have been fearfully linked to death, probably as a result of their association with the witch trials but also due to their ties to ancient predator animal deities around the world and to ancient gods and goddesses of the Underworld.

In Estonian folklore, the returning souls of dead humans, called "home wanderers," or "revenants" could appear in human or animal form. According to Estonian folklorist Eha Viluoja, out of 92 reported instances of "home wanderer" observations, cats (black of course) accounted for 17 of them. Dogs were the primary ghostly object seen, accounting for 35 cases. [120]

Any cat that jumped over a body awaiting burial was a sure sign of bad luck and immediately killed. It was believed that should a cat do such a thing the corpse would rise up to become a vampire.[121]

Regardless if the cat is empowered with evil forces, it has been used to affect folk-cures and to provide protection—in rather strange ways. Folklorist Luc Lacourcière noted that in French Canada it was not uncommon to attempt to transfer disease from the human patient to an animal. In the case of shingles, a skinned-cat was applied to the human body so that the disease could be absorbed into the body of the dead cat.[122]

---

[119] Thompson, C.J.S. *The Hand of Destiny.* New York: Bell Publishing Company 1989, 201.

[120] Viluoja, Eha. "Manifestations of the Revenant in Estonian Folk Tradition", in Folklore, Vol. 2. http://www.folklore.ee/folklore/vol2/viluoja.htm 8/14/06

[121] Guiley, Rosemary Ellen. *The Encyclopedia of Witches & Witchcraft.* New York: Checkmark Books/Facts on File 1999, 49

[122] Lacourcière, Luc. "A Survey of Folk Medicine in French Canada from Early Times to the Present", in *American Folk Medicine*, edited by Wayland D. Hand. Berkeley: University of California Press 1976, 212.

Other treatments include making the sign of the cross with a cat's tail over an eye afflicted with a sty. This reportedly will make the sty disappear. This treatment was used in such diverse areas as Louisiana and England. [123] It was not reported if the cat was living or dead when its tail was used for this purpose. A broth, made from a black cat, was also consumed to cure consumption.

The mystic power of the cat was continuously sought until well into the 19th and 20th century and, most likely, into the 21st century as well. Folk-medicine practices around the world abound in strange rituals to cure certain diseases or to warn individuals away from potentially dangerous events. Many of these today seem naïve and childish—as well as cruel for the poor animals involved. In Oregon in the 1960s folklore warned, "Never allow a child to play with cats or he will become a simpleton." A similar prohibition was reported in Ohio in the 1950s, "If a boy plays with cats, it will make him stupid, for the cat's brain will go into him." [124]

Other dangers associated with playing with cats include the very real possibility of women becoming pregnant (recorded in Oslo during the 1930s). While some folklore warns against being overly friendly with cats the reverse was also true during the 1950s in the American Midwest. "If you make enemies of cats during your lifetime," it was reported, "you will be accompanied to the grave by storms of wind and rain." [125]

Other folk-medicine traditions include one from Germany during the early 20th century that said that thieves could

---

[123] Simpson, Jacqueline and Steve Roud. *Oxford Dictionary of English Folklore.* Oxford: Oxford University Press 2000, 50 and Elizabeth Brandon. "Folk Medicine in French Louisiana" in *American Folk Medicine.* Edited by Wayland D. Hand. Berkeley: University of California Press 1976, 200.
[124] UCLA Folkmedicine Record Numbers 10_4587, 11_4890.
[125] Ibid, Record Number 5_5244

become invisible by cutting off the tips of the tongue of black cats and dogs, "wrap them in wax of an Easter candle, and carry them under the left arm." [126]

A rather grisly tradition in Christian England included sacrificing a cat to ward off evil forces when buildings were constructed. Originally cats, and other animals as well as humans in prehistoric times, were killed and buried in building foundations as sacrifices to the gods and spirits to ensure protection of the structure. Over time, the "sacrificial" aspect was rationalized. Archaeologist Ralph Merrifield wrote, "the cruel practice of killing a cat as a builder's sacrifice was revived by the notion that the body of a cat set in a lifelike attitude in a hidden place would frighten vermin from the building."[127] What the actual "vermin" were is questionable however. Were rodents the focus of these efforts or was it more the spiritual "rodent"—demons and witches—that were the objects of such fear? In some instances a dead cat was found with a single rat in its mouth or near a paw.

While this use of "charms" was widespread across England from the 15th to 19th centuries it also occurred in other locations such as Gibraltar and Sweden.

The importance that the ancient Egyptians placed on cat amulets is described by Howey:

> There are...bronze feline images of various sizes, some engraved with necklace and scarab, others with necklace, and eyes inlaid with gold; figures of cats represented in various stones, in crystal, blue marble, glazed ware and porcelain, exquisite groups of cats and kittens, cat amulets

---

[126] Hoffman-Krayer, Eduard von and Hanns Bächtold-Stäubli, eds. *Handwörterbuch des deutschen Aberglaubens.* Berlin & Leipzig 1927-1942, vol. 2, 235.
[127] Merrifield, Ralph. *The Archaeology of Ritual and Magic.* New York: New Amsterdam Books 1987, 186

of different sizes which had been suspended around the owner's neck in his lifetime, finger-rings of gold on which are engraved the form of the cat, even a child's wooden toy, representing a cat with moveable jaw... [128]

Toads and frogs. One either likes them or is repulsed by them. Regardless of preference they have been incorporated in magic and religion for thousands of years. Frogs have been connected with witches because they were associated with Hecate — the goddess of witches. Frogs were also sacred to the Roman goddess Venus, who is another aspect of Hecate. Heket, the Egyptian Hecate, was a frog goddess "who assisted in fashioning the child in the womb and who presided over its birth."[129] As a sacred midwife, Hecate was depicted in Egyptian art as a frog or as a woman with a frog's head. Amulets of the goddess were simply in the image of frogs but were inscribed, "I am the Resurrection". [130] Babylonian cylinder seals depicted nine frogs as a fertility charm, the frogs representing the Ninefold Goddess that ruled the nine months of gestation.

As Hecate's amulets indicated that she is synonymous with resurrection, so too is the frog which represents her. The frog also came to be regarded as the protector of mothers and newborn children in Egyptian society, and represented fertility, new life, abundance and the embryonic powers of water. The frog's association with fertility was also accepted in the Graeco-Roman world.

---

[128] Howey, M. Oldfield. *The Cat in Magic, Mythology, and Religion.* New York: Crescent Books 1989, 147.
[129] Wilkinson, Richard H. *The Complete Gods and Goddesses of Ancient Egypt.* Lonson: Thames and Hudson Ltd. 2003, 229.
[130] Budge, Sir E.A. Wallis. *Egyptian Magic.* New York: Dover Publications Inc. 1971, 63.

The toad was also sacred to the Lithuanian Goddess of Death and Regeneration, Ragana. As Gimbutas wrote, "If not properly treated, the toad, it was believed even in the early 20th century, can be as dangerous as the Goddess herself." [131]

These dangers included spitting on the toad, which would result in death for the spitter, making the toad angry enough so that it explodes, releasing a deadly poison, and killing the toad with one's bare hands, which changes the killer's face to resemble that of the toad. "As a messenger of death," Gimbutas writes, "the toad can crawl onto the chest of a sleeping person and suck the breath from his or her body, causing certain death." [132] However, the toad is also known for its healing aspects. This is not contradictory at all as both death and regeneration are qualities of Ragana and thusly of the toad.

"The Goddess [of Regeneration] in the form of a frog or toad," Gimbutas tells us, "predominates in the temples, and her icons or amulets...are found throughout the Neolithic, Bronze Age, and even throughout historical times. Beliefs in the body's 'traveling womb' in the form of a frog occur widely from Egypt, Greece, and Rome, to northern Europe during the historical period and, in some places, to this day." [133]

Votive pits uncovered in Danebury and in Aquitane indicate the ritual use of frogs and toads in Celtic traditions. In Danebury, twenty bones of seven species of frogs and toads were found in one pit and in Aquitane a 1st century BCE cremation of toads was discovered. [134] A Roman cemetery uncovered on St. Clare Street in London revealed a 1st or 2nd

---

[131] Gimbutas, Marija. *The Language of the Goddess*. San Francisco: HarperSanFrancisco 1991, 256.
[132] Ibid.
[133] Gimbutas, Marija. *The Civilization of the Goddess: The World of Old Europe*. San Francisco: HarperSanFrancisco 1991, 244.
[134] Green, Miranda. *The Gods of the Celts*. Gloucester: Alan Sutton 1986, 186.

century deposit of eighty frogs or toads along with two broken and two complete flagons suggesting that libations were left along with the frogs and toads as an offering. [135] Frogs were sacred to the Celts for their powers of healing the frog was the Lord of the Earth to the Celts and represented the power of healing water. While frogs and toads may be associated with witches, they are also associated with fairies that may appear as frogs. Three guardian fairies that appear as frogs protect a healing well in Shropshire, England. As frogs and toads were utilized as votive offerings, they were also used for individual spells to harm others. Archaeologist Ralph Merrifield noted, "A black pipkin covered with a slate on which the name 'Nanney Roberts' was written was found buried in a bank on Penrhos Bradwen Farm, near Holyhead, Angelsey, in the nineteenth century; it contained the skin and bones of a frog, which had been pierced by several large pins, and was clearly intended as the image-substitute of the woman named." [136] This particular frog was sacrificed as a curse in relatively recent times.

Frogs were also associated with water and rainmaking in Mesoamerica. As Rands noted "Frogs and toads are generally thought to have a 'natural' connection with rainfall." [137] During the *chac-chaac* rainmaking ceremony of the Maya, frog "impersonators" would mimic their croaking to add power to the rainmaking efforts. "Frogs and snakes," Rands continued "were kept in a pool at the feet of an image of Tlaloc [god of

---

[135] Merrifield, Ralph. *The Archaeology of Ritual and Magic.* New York: New Amsterdam Books 1987, 36. Other offerings in the same pit included a heron, shrews and voles.
[136] Ibid, 155.
[137] Rands, Robert L. "Some Manifestations of Water in Mesoamerican Art," Anthropological Papers, No. 48, Bureau of American Ethnology Bulletin 157. Washington: Smithsonian Institution 1955, 360.

rain and lightning] and during a dance in the god's honor were caught in the mouth and swallowed." [138]

Perhaps the croaking of frogs did result in rain. Zuni lore states, "When frogs warble, they herald rain. The louder the frog, the more rain would fall. When frogs croak much, it is a sign of rain." [139]

In Vedic myth, a giant frog supported the world, as Saunders noted, this was "a metaphor for the primal state of matter." [140]

Carved images of toads, like tortoises, were incorporated in some of the massive altars of Postclassic Mayan temples. These altars were usually placed in front of stelae and were an early part of the Maya stela-altar complex. [141] That the toad was regarded as an important sacred-fertility icon in Mayan society cannot be doubted. "In recently discovered Early Classic stucco reliefs from Balamkú, Campeche," Miller and Taube write, "there are full-figure toads with upwardly facing heads. Seated lords are positioned in their mouths, as if the toads were metaphorically giving birth to the kings." [142]

While frogs were thought to have a natural link to water and to rains it was also believed to be responsible for draught. In both Australia and North America, mythic tales were told of a giant frog swallowing all the waters, creating drought and famine.

Among the Cherokee Indians, it was believed in the past that the "great frog" was responsible for solar eclipses as it

---

[138] Ibid, 361.
[139] Inwards, Richard. *Weather Lore.* London: Elliot Stock 1893, 145.
[140] Saunders, Nicholas J. *Animal Spirits.* London: Duncan Baird Publishers 1997, 106.
[141] Miller, Mary and Karl Taube. *An Illustrated Dictionary of The Gods and Symbols of Ancient Mexico and the Maya.* London: Thames and Hudson 1993, 168.
[142] Ibid.

attempted to swallow the sun. James Mooney tells us "in former times it was customary on such occasions to fire guns and make other loud noises to frighten away the frog." [143] In Mongolia, earthquakes were said to be the result of a giant frog jumping across the land.

The frog in Apache lore was classified as a snake. Frogs were not eaten, as it was believed that anyone who ate a frog would "walk like a cowboy" [i.e. bowlegged]. [144]

The frog was an important mythic figure to the Indian tribes living in the Great Basin and appeared in various locations depicted in rock art. The ability of frogs and other small reptiles to crawl in and out of the cracks and breaks in rocks or to jump in and out of bodies of water "is analogous to a shaman's entry into the supernatural by metaphorically entering either a rock or a spring." [145] Frogs, then, were believed to be the messengers between our physical world and the world of the supernatural. The frog was often carved or painted on stone to represent the trance state of the shaman. The image of the frog was symbolic of going underwater and thereby of death.

An interesting aside is that many of the early Olmec depictions of the were-jaguar may have been of toads instead. The jaguar eventually became an extremely important shamanic animal as well as a prominent god in Mesoamerican religions.

---

[143] Mooney, James. *Myths of the Cherokee*. New York: Dover Publications, Inc. 1995, 306. A reprint of the 1900 publication "Nineteenth Annual Report of the Bureau of American Ethnology, 1897-98.

[144] Opler, Morris Edward. *An Apache Lifeway: The Economic, Social, and Religious Institutions of the Chiricahua Indians.* Chicago: The University of Chicago Press 1941, 332.

[145] Whitley, David S. *A Guide to Rock Art Sites: Southern California and Southern Nevada.* Missoula: Mountain Press Publishing Company 1996, 20.

Frogs and toads were often associated with witches during the Burning Times as witches' familiars—or as forms that witches were able to transform into. One witch trial held in 1665 for Rose Cullender and Amy Duny of Lowestoft, England was concerned with the bewitchment of a child. According to Robin Briggs, "One of the sick child's blankets was hung up and anything found in it thrown into the fire. A toad obligingly appeared and exploded when put in the fire, after which the suspect was discovered much scorched." [146]

Medieval Christians believed that toads were "familiars of witches, symbols of avarice and lust, and tormentors of those in Hell for these and other sins." [147]

Frog superstitions, of which there are many, include the following:

> "In some parts of the country a frog was supposed to possess the soul of a dead child, and it was very unlucky therefore to kill one. The origin…probably lies in the cry of the frog if injured, which is almost human in its note." [148]

Others include the belief that cancer could be cured by swallowing a young frog. Evidently, it was thought that the frog could draw the poison of cancer into its body and eliminate the disease from human victims.

To the Christians the frog represented resurrection but also sin, evil, worldly pleasure, envy and heretics. But then, most symbols originating in ancient times became symbols of evil under Christian influence.

---

[146] Briggs, Robin. *Witches & Neighbors: The Social and Cultural Context of European Witchcraft.* New York: Viking 1996, 209.
[147] Saunders, op cit.
[148] Radford, Edwin and Mona A. *Encyclopaedia of Superstitions.* New York: The Philosophical Library 1949, 127.

Strangely enough, the toad has a much darker position in European folklore than the frog. In sixteenth century, England the toad was regarded as an emissary of the Evil One and often was burned to death. Likewise, the people of Norway believed that the toad was evil, or the representative of evil and they cast unlucky frogs and toads into bonfires that had previously been used by people to dance around and jump over on St. John's Eve. This act of toad killing was believed to ward off trolls and other evil spirits that were active on that night.

While the toad, like the frog, was regarded as a symbol of resurrection, it was also believed to represent other, less desirable things. In Iranian, Celtic and Christian lore the toad represents evil and death. And we cannot forget that Judeo-Christian lore tells of the plague of frogs that was visited upon Pharaoh.

The toad, however, like many other sacred symbols, has a dual nature. A general piece of folklore from the 1940s said, "If a toad crosses the path of a bridal party on the way to church, the couple will have prosperity and happiness." The Araucanian and Orinoco Indians of Chile and Venezuela called the toad the Lord of the Water and the toad was believed to watch over the preservation of water. Its link to water, like the frog's association to water, was a common belief. In Lincolnshire, England, toads were kept in household wells to ensure the water's purity and much effort was taken to ensure that the toad never escaped from its well enclosure.

Another common bit of lore from Herefordshire was "If you wear a toad's heart concealed on your person, you can steal to your heart's content without being found out." I wonder how many boys were amazed at being caught even though they had a toad's heart in their pocket?

In 1892, a severe outbreak of flu ravaged Togo and it was blamed on evil spirits. To expel the spirits and remove the disease "they dragged a toad through the streets, followed by an elder scattering holy water. By this means the epidemic was concentrated in the toad, which was then cast into the nearby forest." [149]

To explore even more in the remote past frogs and toads were regarded as sacred and often were associated with goddesses. Frog-woman hybrid figures were common in Anatolia dating back to the 6th millennium BCE. Symbols of regeneration, these figures had human heads and vulvas but with a decidedly frog-like body. Such figures were etched and carved in marble, alabaster, clay, ceramics, and stone since early Neolithic times. Some of the earliest carved forms have perforations that obviously imply that they were worn as amulets.

Other animals such as the snake, owl, bat, the turtle and the eagle have been regarded as clan and individual totems as well and much of the world's mythology and folklore has originated from the people who have worshipped and feared them.

"The snake is a main image of the vitality and continuity of life," wrote anthropologist Marija Gimbutas, "the guarantor of life energy in the home, and the symbol of family and animal life."[150] The snake means something different and yet the same in many cultures and locations. The serpent is a feared goddess of the river, a messenger and spirit being of Native America, a water spirit and god of Africa. These are similar characteristics for a universally important symbol. There is an opposite view, however. The snake is also

---

[149] Radford, op cit 241.
[150] Gimbutas, Marija. *The Civilization of the Goddess: The World of Old Europe*. San Francisco: HarperSanFrancisco 1991, 236.

portrayed as Satan himself in Biblical lore. As historian Jean Markale wrote, "Western religious thought has been almost unanimous in making the serpent of Genesis into a concrete representation of the tempter, that is to say, of Satan himself, relying for support upon the Apocalypse where this 'great serpent'...is the image of absolute evil." [151] The serpent had been respected as a symbol of wisdom and life renewed for thousands of years—until the Hebrews and then the Christians waged successful campaigns to destroy it. "When the Hebrews introduced a male god into Canaan," says Mark O'Connell and Raje Airey, "the female deity and the snake were relegated and associated with evil." [152] Later, the Christian campaign was able to, as Page Bryant wrote, "distort a positive and ancient pagan symbol to suit the purposes of Christianity." [153]

Even before Christianity established a toehold the serpent was viewed by the Hebrews as either possessed by Satan or was Satan himself. In Jewish folklore, the original serpent walked on two legs, talked and ate the same food that Adam and Eve did. One day the serpent witnessed Adam and Eve engaged in sexual relations, and he became jealous—persuading Eve to eat the forbidden fruit. In punishment, according to Hebrew legend, "its hands and legs were cut off, so it had to crawl on its belly, all food it ate tasted of dust, and it became the eternal enemy of man." [154] However, the serpent also was able to have sexual relations with Eve before he was punished by God. Because of this the Israelites only became

---

[151] Markale, Jean. *The Great Goddess: Reverence of the Devine Feminine From the Paleolithic to the Present.* Rochester: Inner Traditions 1999, 6.
[152] O'Connell, Mark and Raje Airey. *The Complete Encyclopedia of Signs & Symbols.* London: Hermes House 2005, 186.
[153] Bryant, Page. *Awakening Arthur!* London: The Aquarian Press 1991, 64
[154] Unterman, Alan. *Dictionary of Jewish Lore & Legend.* New York: Thames and Hudson 1991, 176.

purified when they stood at Mt. Sinai and received the torah. "Gentiles, however," according to Alan Untermann, "have never been cleansed of this serpentine impurity." [155]

Christian hatred of the serpent was not universal however. In Armenian folklore, according to Anthony S. Mercatante, "Christ himself is identified with Shahapet, a beneficient serpent spirit who inhabited olive trees and vinestocks in the ancient mythology." [156]

A graven image of a serpent suspended from a cross-like beam was erected by Moses to protect the Hebrews from the poisonous bite of serpents. Acting on God's instructions, "…Moses made a serpent of brass, and put it upon a pole, and it came to pass, that if a serpent had bitten any man, when he beheld the serpent of brass, he lived." [157]

On the base of one of the ancient menhirs in Carnac an image of five snakes standing on their tails was carved. "When the site was excavated," writes archaeologist Johannes Maringer, "in 1922, five axes were found under the engravings. The blades faced upward; obviously the axes had been deliberately placed in that position. It is most likely that even in Neolithic times the serpent was a symbol of life." [158] Maringer believes that the serpent was closely associated with deceased ancestors and the five serpents engraved on the menhir probably indicated that five people were buried there along with the axes.

The duality of meanings most likely originated in the contrasting views of the serpent in Old European and Indo-European mythology. In Old European lore (prior to 4500

---

[155] Ibid.
[156] Mercatante, Anthony S. *Good and Evil in Myth & Legend.* New York: Barnes & Noble 1978, 65.
[157] Numbers 21:9, KJV
[158] Maringer, Johannes. *The Gods of Prehistoric Man: History of Religion.* London: Phoenix Press 2002, 170-171.

BCE) the serpent was benevolent, a symbol of life and fertility in both plants and animals (including humans), protective of the family and of domestic livestock. "Snakes are guardians of the springs of life and immortality," wrote Spanish scholar J.E. Cirlot, "and also of those superior riches of the spirit that are symbolized by hidden treasure." [159] The poisonous snake in Old European lore was, according to Gimbutas, "an epiphany of the Goddess of Death". [160] Indo-European mythology (evolving between 4000 and 2500 BCE) contrasted this view, regarding the snake as a symbol of evil, an epiphany of the God of Death, and an adversary of the Thunder God. This was the point in time that the Goddess religion began to give way to that of the male dominated religion of the Sky God.

Gimbutas goes on to say, "it is not the body of the snake that was sacred, but the energy exuded by this spiraling or coiling creature which transcends its boundaries and influences the surrounding world." [161]

In the Classic world the serpent was the creator of the universe, it laid the Cosmic Egg and split it asunder to form the heavens and the earth. As Hans Leisgang wrote, "This serpent, which coiled round the heavens, biting its tail, was the cause of solar and lunar eclipses. In the Hellenistic cosmology, this serpent is assigned to the ninth, starless spheres of the planets and the zodiac. This sphere goes round the heavens and the earth and also under the earth, and governs the winds." [162] "In Christian theology," Leisegang

---

[159] Cirlot. J. E. *A Dictionary of Symbols, 2nd Edition.* New York: Barnes & Noble Books 1995, 286.
[160] Gimbutas, op cit, 400.
[161] Gimbutas, Marija. *The Language of the Goddess.* San Francisco: HarperSanFrancisco 1991, 121.
[162] Leisegang, Hans. "The Mystery of the Serpent" in *Pagan and Christian Mysteries: Papers from the Eranos Yearbook*, edited by Joseph Campbell.

continues, "this serpent became the prince of the world, the adversary of the transcendental God, the dragon of the outer darkness, who has barred off this world from above, so that it can be redeemed only by being annihilated." [163]

This creator-serpent, the Great Serpent, was symbolic of the sun, not evil but "the good spirit of light" as Leisegang so aptly describes it. It is this Great Serpent that is cause and ruler of the four seasons, the four winds and the four quarters of the cosmos.

A white snake, like the salmon, was a source for wisdom and magical power and was associated with the goddess/Saint Brigit, also known in England and Scotland as Bride. On February 1st, Bride's Day the serpent woke for its winter hibernation to bring in the change in seasons from winter to spring. Mackinzie relates an old Gaelic charm:

"To-day is the day of Bride,
The serpent shall come from his hole;
I will not molest the serpent
And the serpent will not molest me."[164]

The many serpent-like symbols found in ancient rock art the world over testify to the importance of this animal in the human mind. The zigzag and meandering lines symbolic of water, the mysterious spirals found the world over which mimic the coiled serpent all speak of the underlying mystery that humans have felt towards the snake and the snakes place in the mythos of the Otherworld and death. However, not

---

New York: The Bollingen Foundation/Harper & Row Publishers 1955, 26-27.
[163] Ibid, 27.
[164] Mackenzie, Donald A. *Ancient Man in Britain*. London: Senate 1996, 188-189. A reprint of the 1922 edition published by Blackie & Son Limited, London.

only death, for many the snake represented life and the renewal of life. The snake was the feared guardian of life and the forces of life as well as the messenger to and from the world of the dead. Snakes were believed to be symbolic of the departed soul to the ancient Greeks. It was also valued as a guardian of temples, treasuries and oracles, its eyesight believed to be especially keen to allow it to effectively guard against intrusion. Joseph Campbell noted that "in India…the 'serpent kings' guard both the waters of immortality and the treasures of the earth." [165]

While many male anthropologists and archaeologists argue that the serpent is symbolic of fertility (as a phallic symbol), art historian Merlin Stone offers another view:

"[The serpent] appears to have been primarily revered as a female in the Near and Middle East and generally linked to wisdom and prophetic counsel rather than fertility and growth as is so often suggested."[166]

This statement is not entirely true. The god Ningiszida ("Lord of the Good Tree") was an important male deity in Mesopotamia. As an underworld god, he was guardian over demons and at least one Sumerian ruler regarded Ningiszida as his personal protector. While primarily a god of the underworld there is one myth ("Adapa at the gate of heaven") that has Ningiszida as one of the guardians at the gates of heaven. [167] "The symbol and beast of Ningiszida," according to Black and Green, "was the horned snake…" [168]

---

[165] Campbell, Joseph. *Creative Mythology: The Masks of God Volume IV.* London: Secker & Warburg 1968, 120.
[166] Stone, Merlin. *When God Was A Woman.* New York: Barnes & Noble Books 1993, 199.
[167] Black, Jeremy and Anthony Green. *Gods, Demons and Symbols of Ancient Mesopotamia.* Austin: University of Texas Press 2000, 139.
[168] Ibid 140.

The snake and the serpent have been depicted as goddesses and gods, as holy beings to be worshipped, as dragons, as devils and as symbols of lust, greed and sin—and of death. In mythic lore, Zeus appears in snake form to mate with Persephone who thereafter gives birth to Dionysos, "the god who in Crete, it so happens, was synonymous with Zeus."[169] The serpent is "the emblem of all self-creative divinities and represents the generative power of the earth. It is solar, chthonic, sexual, funerary and the manifestation of force at any level, a source of all potentialities both material and spiritual," writes J.C. Cooper, "and closely associated with the concepts of both life and death." [170]

The Giants of classic Greek and Roman mythology reportedly had snake-like legs as did the founder of Athens, Cecrops. Cecrops, a semi-serpent, was considered an innovator of his day, abolishing blood sacrifice, introducing basic laws of marriage, politics and property and encouraging the worship of Zeus and Athena. [171] Again, a duality exists between these two creatures with snake-like characteristics. The Giants were enemies of Zeus and were defeated by Hercules on behalf of the gods of Olympus and Cecrops was a champion for the causes of Zeus.

Recent excavations in the Kenar Sandal area in Jiroft, Iran have uncovered additional serpent-legged figures. According to the *Persian Journal*,[172] the reliefs depicting two men with

---

[169] Baring, Anne and Jules Cashford. *The Myth of the Goddess: Evolution of an Image*. London: Arkana/Penguin Books 1991, 317.
[170] Cooper, J.C. *An Illustrated Encyclopaedia of Traditional Symbols*. London : Thames and Hudson 1978, 147.
[171] Cotterell, Arthur. *The Encyclopedia of Mythology: Classical, Celtic, Greek*. London: Hermes House 2005, 84.
[172] "New Stone Reliefs Discovered in Jiroft, Iran" in *Persian Journal*, February 2, 2006.
http://www.iranian.ws/iran_news/publish/article_12873.shtml

"snake tails instead of legs" were carved on soapstone on a "flat stone cliff." At one time almost 5,000 years ago, Kenar Sandal was an important trade city for the Persian Gulf region, linking what is now present day Afghanistan, Pakistan, Iran and Tajikistan. The serpent-men reliefs indicate that this image has an ancient origin most likely outside the classic Greco-Roman world.

Zeus conquers the Serpent-legged Titans

In support of the view that this mythic creature originated in the non-Classic World are the serpent-men of the Indian Underworld, the "demonic Cobras" called the Nagas. According to Mackenzie "they are of human form to the waist, the rest of their bodies being like those of serpents." [173] The Nagas were demi-gods to the Indian serpent worshippers and were, according to Mackenzie, "occasionally 'the friends

---

[173] Mackenzie, Donald A. *India Myths & Legends*. London: Studio Editions 1993, 65.

of man', and to those they favoured they gave draughts of their nectar, which endowed them with great strength." [174]

Abrasax Gem Amulet

An interesting image similar to the serpent-legged Titans and the Nagas is that carved upon the strange "Abrasax gems", magical amulets introduced in the second century that mingled early Christian and Pagan themes. Originating in Alexandria, the images most certainly were inspired by the mystic powers of the man-serpent as represented by the Titans.

It is interesting to note that Athens has even more connections to serpent-men in the form of Erichthonius—the first king of Athens. According to legend, this serpent being was created from the semen of the smith-god Hephaistos. Hephaistos had attempted to rape Athena but she miraculously disappeared just in time. His semen, as it fell to the earth, grew into the serpent Erichthonius. Ely offers an

---

[174] Ibid., 66.

alternative view: "In the days of Pausanias, Hephaistos and Gaia were said to be the parents of Erichthonius." This version evidently arose from the more conservative elements of Greek society that could not abide with the original creation of the serpent-being from an act of rape. [175]

In Mesoamerican traditions, the Plumed Serpent, Quetzalcoatl, called "the wise instructor," brings culture and knowledge to the people and "takes charge or interferes in creative activities" of the world. [176] It is Quetzalcoatl who discovers corn and provides it for humankind's nourishment. While historical lore indicates that Quetzalcoatl was a man (in fact, a tall, white man with a beard), he is symbolically represented as a serpent on many temple complexes, the most notable being at Chichen-Itza in Yucatan. During certain times of the year the steps the lead up the pyramid temple cast an undulating shadow that connects with the carved stone serpent heads—bringing to life the Plumed Serpent.

The serpent also represents chaos, corruption and darkness along with knowledge and spirit. It is this knowledge that the Bible uses to evict Adam and Eve from paradise and what brings the snake so much hatred. It is the symbolism of the snake, that is so closely associated with the Earth and the Earth's creative powers that the followers of the Sky God wished to destroy. According to Andrews, the snake "threatened the world order established by the sky gods and continually tried to return the world to its original state of chaos."[177]

---

[175] Ely, Talfourd. *The Gods of Greece and Rome.* Mineola: Dover Publications Inc. 2003, 161. A reprint of the 1891 edition published by G.P. Putnam's Sons, New York.
[176] Bierhorst, John. *The Mythology of Mexico and Central America.* New York: William Morrow and Company 1990, 145.
[177] Andrews, Tamra. *A Dictionary of Nature Myths.* Oxford: Oxford University Press 1998, 176.

The serpent, in fact, threatened the order and control of the Judeo-Christian religion. As Markale suggests, Eve disobeyed the patriarchal priests and listened to the serpent, the serpent being representative of the Mother Goddess. "This is a case, pure and simple, of a return to the mother-goddess cult, a true 'apostasy' as it were, and thus a very grave sin against the patriarchal type of religion that Yahweh represents."[178] Markale and others, most notably the French Catholic priest André de Smet, believe that the original sin was the first battle in the long struggle between the patriarchal religion of Yahew and the matriarchal religion of the Mother Goddess. The "curse against the serpent," Markale writes, "…is against the mother goddess herself." [179]

The Gnostic writers viewed the serpent in a different manner. The Kabbalist Joseph Gikatila wrote in his book *Mystery of the Serpent*:

"Know and believe that the Serpent, at the beginning of creation, was indispensable to the order of the world, so long as he kept his place; and he was a great servent…and he was needed for the ordering of all the chariots, each in its place…It is he who moves the spheres and turns them from East to the West and from North to the South. Without him there would have been neither seed nor germination, nor will to produce any created thing."[180]

The Ophites, a successor group of the original Gnostics, venerated the snake. To the Ophites the serpent was made by God to be "the cause of Gnosis for mankind…It was the serpent…who taught man and woman the complete knowledge of the mysteries on high" which resulted in the

---

[178] Markale, op cit, 6.
[179] Ibid, 7.
[180] As quoted by Jean Doresse, *The Secret Books of the Egyptian Gnostics*. New York: MJF Books 1986, 292-293.

serpent being "cast down from the heavens." [181] To this group the snake was the "living symbol of the celestial image that they worshipped."[182] According to Doresse, the Ophites kept and fed serpents in special baskets and conducted their meetings near the serpent's burrows. Doresse wrote, "They arranged loaves of bread upon a table, and then, by means of incantations, they allured the snake until it came coiling its way among these offerings; and only then, did they partake of the bread, each one kissing the muzzle of the reptile they had charmed. This, they claimed, was the perfect sacrifice, the true Eucharist."[183] To the Gnostic Christians, serpent worship was associated with the "restoration of Paradise, and release thereby from the bondages of time." [184]

A similar ritual has taken place each August 15th on the Greek island of Kefalonia. On this day, also known as the feast of the Falling Asleep of the Virgin, in the small village of Markopoulo, small snakes with a small cross-like mark on their heads slither through a churchyard, emerging near the bell tower and make their way toward the church. According to witnesses, the snakes enter the church building through bell rope holes in the wall; crawl over the furniture and even over the worshippers as they sit in the pews. The snakes continue onward to the bishop's throne and, as a group, to the icon of the Virgin.

After the service, the serpents disappear and not seen again until the same evening a year later. The people of Markopoulo look forward to the appearance of these creatures as a sign of good luck and bountiful harvests. Only two years in recent memory did not see the return of the

---

[181] Ibid, 44.
[182] Ibid, 45.
[183] Ibid, 44.
[184] Campbell, op cit. 151.

snakes. One was in 1940. The next year Greece was invaded by the Axis Forces. The year following their non-appearance in 1953 saw the area devastated by a catastrophic earthquake.

Normally avoiding human contact during their visits to the church the snakes appear quite tame and allow the residents to handle them at will. According to local lore, the annual serpent appearance dates to 1705 when Barbarossa pirates attacked the village. The nuns who resided in the village convent prayed to the Virgin to transform them into snakes to avoid being captured by the pirates, or worse. When the pirates finally gained access to the convent, they were shocked to see the floors, walls and icons writhing with snakes. The snakes have returned each year except for the two previously mentioned.

The serpent, as a representative of the mother goddess, is known from the serpent priestesses of Crete and various other mother goddess locations from the Neolithic. The shrine at Gournia, Crete yielded three figures of the mother goddess. One that shows the mother goddess with a serpent curled around her waist and over one shoulder.[185] The Greek mother goddess Ge or Gaia is often associated with the "earth snake."

Twenty-one figurines of serpent goddesses have been found at Poduri, Romania dating from 4800 to 4600 BCE indicating that this goddess was not only an ancient one but commonly worshiped throughout Europe and the Middle East. Archaeologist Marija Gimbutas wrote "Their lack of arms, their snake-shaped heads, and the snakes coiling over their abdomens suggest that they represent the Snake

---

[185] Mackenzie, Donald A. *Myths and Legends Crete & Pre-Hellenic.* London: Senate 1995, 261. A reprint of the 1917 edition published as *Crete & Pre-Hellenic Europe* by The Gresham Publishing Company, London.

Goddess and her attendants, only one of them has an arm raised to her face, a gesture of power." [186]

"Undulating serpents or dragons signify cosmic rhythm, or the power of the waters." [187] The serpent has been associated with water since time began. They appear in Native American rock art throughout the continent symbolic of messengers of the otherworld that traverse through streams, rivers and time through the cracks in stone. It is by no accident that the Plumed Serpent of Mesoamerica is closely associated with the Cosmic Waters or that the Serpent Mound in the Ohio Valley is located near a flowing river. It is also not an accident that accounts of sea serpents are rampant in the world's maritime lore. In the Southwest, snakes were pecked or painted onto rock surfaces designating good or bad water sources. The snake was believed by Native Americans, as well as to the people of Old Europe and the ancient Near East, to bring rain when it is needed. Both the Hopi and Shasta Indians carried live snakes in their mouths for ritual dances used in rainmaking ceremonies[188] and the Cheyenne also danced with poisonous snakes in their "crazy dances". "Crazy dances" were performed to aid in the cure of a sick child, to ensure victory in war or to obtain other blessings for the tribe.[189]

Snakes have also contributed to weather folklore around the world associated with rain. Nineteenth century folklorist Richard Inwards noted, "the chief characteristic of the serpents throughout the East in all ages seems to have been their power over the wind and rain, which they gave or

---

[186] Gimbutas, op cit, 343.
[187] Cooper, op cit, 148.
[188] Kasner, Leone Letson. *Spirit Symbols in Native American Art.* Philomath: Ayers Mountain Press 1992, 113.
[189] Mooney, James. *The Ghost-Dance Religion and the Sioux Outbreak of 1890.* Chicago: The University of Chicago Press 1965, 273.

withheld, according to their good or ill will towards man."[190] It was also possible to induce rain, according to Inwards, by hanging a dead snake on a tree. [191]

Mesoamerican traditions "have been recorded," writes anthropologist Robert Rands, "which directly connect the serpent with surface water, rain, and lightning. ...a few stray facts regarding the relationship of snakes to the anthropomorphic rain deities of the Maya and Mexicans may be noted. In the Maya codices, the serpent...and water are frequently shown together...As giant celestial snakes or as partly anthropomorphized serpents, the Chicchans are rain and thunder deities of the present-day Chorti. ...In modern Zoque belief, snakes serve as the whips of the thunderbolts." [192]

The snake with its fluid motions is a natural symbol of flowing water. Native Americans and others saw this symbolism in the meandering streams and rivers that flow through their lands. They also saw the annual shedding of its skin as a renewal of life and of fertility, a renewal of the fertility that water also provides.

"The serpent is the foundation of the universe," writes Indian artist Jyoti Sahi. "Coiled around the naval of the cosmos, it appears to be the dynamic centre of time and space. The serpent seems always to be moving and yet always still, like the oceans whose waves seem in perpetual turmoil and unrest, but whose boundaries remain fixed, and whose depths are eternal." [193]

---

[190] Inwards, Richard. *Weather Lore*. London: Elliot Stock 1893.
[191] Ibid.
[192] Rands, Robert L. "Some Manifestations of Water in Mesoamerican Art," Anthropological Papers, No. 48, Bureau of American Ethnology Bulletin 157. Washington: Smithsonian Institution 1955, 361, pgs 265-393.
[193] Sahi, Jyoti. *The Child and the Serpent: Reflections on Popular Indian Symbols*. London: Arkana/Penguin Books 1980, 161.

In ancient Indian mythology, the serpent becomes the victim of mankind, "...in order to overcome the wilderness...and make it orderly and cultivated...[man] had to injure the serpent..." [194] Sahi says that this injury to the serpent is a "sin" and that the story really "represents the overthrowing of pre-Aryan serpent worship." [195]

In the ancient Mesopotamian city of Ur, the snake god Irhan was worshipped. To these people Irhan was representative of the Euphrates River. The mildly poisonous horned vipers of the Middle East gradually assumed the dragon form that we still recognize today.

A snake-dragon called *mušhuššu*, or "furious snake" was worshipped in Babylon at least during the reign of Nebuchadnezzar II (604 to 562 BCE). This creature with the body and neck of a serpent, lion's forelegs and a bird's hindlegs, was originally an attendant of the city god Ninazu of Ešnunna. The snake-dragon was transferred as an attendant of Ninazu to several other national gods through the years, surviving as a protective pendant through the Hellenistic Period. [196]

The serpent was present in the liturgy and symbolism of the Mithraic religion as well. Mithraism almost dominated Christianity during the 2nd and 3rd centuries and many Christian symbols are derived from this ancient religion. The snake appears often in paintings and carvings of Mithras with the serpent presented as a companion to the god. Some depict the serpent seeking the flowing sacrificial blood of the bull that was slain in Mithraic baptisms. This, according to writer

---

[194] Ibid, 165.
[195] Ibid, 166.
[196] Jeremy and Anthony Green. *Gods, Demons and Symbols of Ancient Mesopotamia*. Austin: University of Texas Press 2000, 166.

D. Jason Cooper, "seems to indicate the snake is seeking salvation."[197]

Mithras and his salvation seeking serpent

Snakes are also associated with healing. The caduceus, the staff with two intertwined serpents, is found not only in the healing temples of Greece, but also in Native American, Mesoamerican and Hindu symbolism. The snake with its annual shedding of its skin was a logical symbol for life, renewal and protection. In Celtic lands as well the snake was, like the sacred well, associated with healing. To the Sumerians the caduceus was the symbol of life. The caduceus was also an important symbol to some Gnostic Christians who, according to Barbara Walker, "worshipped the serpent hung on a cross…or Tree of Life, calling it Christ the Savior, also a title of Hermes the Wise Serpent represented by his own holy

---

[197] Cooper, D. Jason. *Mithras: Mysteries and Initiation Rediscovered.* York Beach: Samuel Weiser, Inc. 1996, 74.

caduceus..." [198] According to Wallis Budge, "the symbol of [the Bablyonian god of healing, Ningishzida] was a staff round which a double-sexed, two-headed serpent called Sachan was coiled, and a form of this is the recognized mark of the craft of the physician at the present day." [199] The Greek god of healing, Aesculapius was also depicted in a statue at Epidaurus "holding a staff in one hand, while his other hand rested on the head of a snake..."[200]

In Africa the spirits of the waters are, simply said, snakes. As they are symbolic of healing, they are also believed to "call" to healers to whom they give wisdom and knowledge.[201] According to anthropologist Penny Bernard, "the water spirits have been attributed a pivotal role in the calling, initiation and final induction of certain diviners in the Eastern Cape. Hence the implication that they are the key to certain forms of 'sacred' knowledge." [202]

Tornadoes and waterspouts were believed to be the physical appearance of the African serpent god Inkanyamba. Inkanyamba was believed to be an enormous serpent that twisted and writhed to and fro as it reached from the earth to the sky. Tamra Andrews noted that the Zulu "believed that he grew larger and larger as he rose out of his pool and then grew smaller and smaller when he retreated back into it." [203]

In other African cultures, the snake is considered the spirit of a departed human. Referred to as the 'living-dead' the

---

[198] Walker, Barbara G. *The Women's Encyclopedia of Myths and Secrets.* Edison: Castle Books 1996, 131.
[199] Budge, E.A. Wallis. *Babylonian Life and History.* New York: Barnes & Noble Books 2005, 167.
[200] Ibid.
[201] Bernard, Penny. "Mermaids, Snakes and the Spirits of the Water in Southern Africa: Implications for River Health", op cit., 3.
[202] Ibid., 4.
[203] Andrews, op cit, 96.

snake is prohibited from being killed, as it is representative of the soul of a relative or friend that is visiting the land of the living. [204]

According to Sumatran and Norse mythology, the vast Cosmic Snake that encircles the world in the cosmic river will eventually destroy it. However from the destruction comes a new world, a renewal of life. The old gods die with the Cosmic Serpent but "Earth will rise again from the waves, fertile, green, and fair as never before, cleansed of all its sufferings and evil."[205]

Perhaps in no other culture than Egypt was the serpent-god so prevalent. The serpent represented both male and female deities, both benign and malevolent. The snake-god Apophis was believed to have existed before time in the primeval chaos of pre-creation. Apophis was the enemy of the sun god and attacked the heavenly ship of Ra as it sojourned across the heavens. The daily battle involved other gods, including Seth the enemy of Osiris, in a back and forth struggle of power between light and dark and balance and chaos. Each day Apophis was defeated, cut into pieces that would revive and rejoin the struggle the next day. In his own way Apophis was a symbol of renewal—renewal brought about by the eternal conflict of the powers of the universe. Apophis was associated with natural disaster, storms, earthquakes and unnatural darkness that foretold the return of chaos. As archaeologist Richard Wilkinson wrote, "Although the god was neither worshipped in a formal cult nor incorporated into popular veneration, Apophis entered

---

[204] Mbiti, John S. *African Religions and Philosophy*. Garden City: Anchor Books 1970, 216.
[205] Davidson, H. R. Ellis. *Gods and Myths of the Viking Age*. New York: Bell Publishing Company 1981, 38.

both spheres of religion as a god or demon to be protected against."[206]

The Egyptians worshiped ten other snake gods. These include Mehen who helped protect Ra from the daily attacks of Apophis, Denwen who was very much like a dragon and had the ability to cause a fiery conflagration, Kebehwet who was a "celestial serpent," Meretseger called the "goddess of the pyramidal peak" and who presided over the necropolis at Thebes. Meretseger became an important deity of the workmen who constructed the burial temples and chambers and many representations of this serpent goddess have been found in workmen's homes and shops in the area.

Other serpent gods of the Egyptians include Nehebu-Kau, "he who harnesses the spirits."[207] Nehebu-Kau was regarded as a helpful deity and was the son of the scorpion goddess Serket. He was referred to in hieroglyph as the "great serpent, multitudinous of coils" and was sometimes depicted as a man with a serpent's head. Other beneficent serpent gods include Renenutet, a guardian of the king and goddess of the harvest and fertility. She was also known as a divine nurse. The cobra goddess Wadjet ("the green one") was a goddess of the Nile Delta and was associated with the world of the living rather than the world of the dead. Wadjet was another protector of the king and had the ability to spit flames as a defensive measure. The serpent on the pharaoh's crown was that of Wadjet. Like Renenutet, Wadjet was also a nurse to the god Hathor while he was yet a divine infant. Another fiery serpent is Wepset. Wepset, meaning "she who burns," guarded the king, other gods and the Eye of Ra. It was written in ancient texts that the Egyptian island of Biga was her cult center.

---

[206] Wilkinson, Richard H. *The Complete Gods and Goddesses of Ancient Egypt.* New York: Thames & Hudson 2003, 223.
[207] Ibid, 224.

The last two Egyptian serpent deities are Weret-Hekau and Yam. "Great of magic" was the name for Weret-Hekau and she may be a composite of other serpent goddesses in that she was also a nursing serpent of the kings and her symbol is associated with the other uraeus goddesses. Yam was actually a Semitic god, a "tyrannical, monstrous deity of the sea", according to Wilkinson.[208] Sometimes depicted as a seven-headed sea monster, Yam was a minor Egyptian god that may have been feared mostly by sailors and fishermen than by regular people of the cities. Yam was defeated in various myths by the goddess Astarte, and the Canaanite god Baal and the Egyptian god Seth.

Serapis, a deity of both the Greeks and Egyptians, associated with Osiris, Hermes, and Hades, was introduced in the 3rd century BCE as a state god for both Greeks and Egyptians. Believed by the Egyptians to be a human manifestation of Apis, a sacred bull that symbolized Osiris, he was represented as a god of fertility and medicine and the ruler of the dead to the Greeks. Serapis was also depicted as a Sun god and occasionally with a serpent wrapped around his body—most likely in connection with fertility.

That serpents were, and still are an extremely important aspect of religious traditions around the world cannot be doubted when even Ireland, a land totally devoid of snakes, is so obsessed with the image of the serpent. "Is it not a singular circumstance," said 19th century scholar Marcus Keane, "that in Ireland where no living serpent exists, such numerous legends of serpents should abound, and that figures of serpents should be so profusely used to ornament Irish sculptures?" [209] Celtic scholar James Bonwick himself noted

---

[208] Ibid, 228.
[209] as quoted by James Bonwick in *Irish Druids and Old Irish Religions*. New York: Barnes & Noble Books 1986, 173. A reprint of the 1894 edition.

when he visited Cashel, Ireland in the 1880s that he saw "a remarkable stone, bearing a nearly defaced sculpture of a female—head and bust—but whose legs were snakes." [210] It was Bonwick's belief that this ancient stone carving depicted an "object of former worship." The "popularity" of the serpent image in Ireland caused Bonwick to write, "That one of the ancient military symbols of Ireland should be a serpent, need not occasion surprise in us. The Druidical serpent of Ireland is perceived in the Tara brooch, popularized to the present day. Irish crosses, so to speak, were alive with serpents." [211]

Serpents were valued in Slavic countries up through the 19th century as good-luck symbols. Snakes were also valued as protective charms in Sweden where they were buried under the foundations of houses and other structures. Russian peasants kept them as pets and, as in Poland; snakes were given food and drink in exchange for their protective charms.

Snakes were associated with an ancient god of thunder in Slavic countries. The thunder god was "responsible for creating mountains and for hurling down bolts of lightning also launched storms of life-giving rain into the earth beneath him." [212] Kerrigan writes "Awesome as his strength was, pagan belief did not characterize it as being wielded destructively: only with the coming of Christianity did his powers become identified with those of evil." [213]

In some Native American lore, the snake was usually considered an animal to be avoided—one of the "bad animals" that was prohibited from journeying to the spirit

---

[210] Ibid 174.
[211] Ibid 168.
[212] Kerrigan, Michael. "A Fierce Menagerie" in *Forests of the Vampire: Slavic Myth*. New York: Barnes & Noble 2003, 124.
[213] Ibid.

world after death. [214] To the Lakota the spirit of the snake "presided over the ability to do things slyly, to go about unknown and unseen, and of lying."[215]

Cherokee shamans prohibited the killing of snakes and the Apache forbid the killing of any snake by their own people but would not hesitate to ask strangers to kill them.[216] The Cherokee generic name for the snake is *inădû'* and they are believed to be supernatural, having close associations with rain and the thunder gods, as well as having a certain influence over other plants and animals. "The feeling toward snakes," wrote James Mooney, "is one of mingled fear and reverence, and every precaution is taken to avoid killing or offending one…"[217] Certain shamans were able to kill rattlesnakes for use in rituals or for medicinal uses. The head was always cut off and buried an arms length deep in the earth. If this was not done, the snake would cause the rain to fall until the streams and rivers overflowed their banks. [218]

Specific snake lore of the Cherokee indicates that some serpents were not only associated with rain, thunder and the supernatural but also were very unlucky. Mooney reported that a large serpent was once said to reside on the north bank of the Little Tennessee and the main Tennessee rivers in Loudon county, Tennessee and it was considered an evil omen simply to see it. "On one occasion," he wrote, "a man

---

[214] Walker, James R. *Lakota Belief and Ritual.* Lincoln: University of Nebraska Press 1991, 71.
[215] Ibid, 122.
[216] Bourke, John G. *Apache Medicine-Men.* New York: Dover Publications, Inc. 1993, 20. A reprint of the1892 edition of *The Medicine-Men of the Apache* published in the Ninth Annual Report of the Bureau of Ethnology to the Secretary of the Smithsonian Institution 1887-88, Washington, pgs 443-603.
[217] Mooney, James. *Myths of the Cherokee.* New York: Dover Publications 1995, 294.
[218] Ibid, 296.

crossing the river...saw the snake in the water and soon afterward lost one of his children." [219]

Illnesses were often thought to be caused by snakes, and even the act of accidentally touching the discarded skin of a snake was believed to cause sickness, especially skin ailments and perhaps even death. [220]

The Apache avoided even mentioning the snake but would sometimes use it as an invective. However, by doing even this one courted disaster. According to Opler, "If a man says in anger, 'I hope a snake bites you,' he will get sick from snakes. ..Before this the snakes have not bothered him, but...it's bound to make him sick." [221]

When a snake is accidentally encountered on a trail, it is, according to Opler, "accorded the greatest respect and is referred to by a relationship term: ..."My mother's father, don't bother me! I'm a poor man. Go where I can't see you. Keep out of my path." [222]

Cherokee lore tells of strange snake-like creatures that were obviously more than myth as no tale of heroes or supernatural interventions are part of the tales. They are simply told as observations and accounts of frightful encounters between men and monster. One such beast is called the Ustû'tlĭ, or "foot snake" which lived on the Cohutta Mountain. Ethnologist James Mooney recorded stories at the beginning of the 20th century about this monster and gives us the following description:

"...it did not glide like other snakes, but had feet at each end of its body, and moved by strides or jerks, like a great

---

[219] Mooney, op cit 414.
[220] Opler, Morris Edward. *An Apache Life-Way: The Economic, Social, and Religious Institutions of the Chiricahua Indians.* Chicago: The University of Chicago Press 1941, 228.
[221] Ibid.
[222] Ibid, 227.

measuring worm. These feet were three-cornered and flat and could hold on to the ground like suckers. It had no legs, but would raise itself up on its hind feet, with its snaky head waving high in the air until it found a good place to take a fresh hold…It could cross rivers and deep ravines by throwing its head across and getting a grip with its front feet and then swinging it body over." [223]

A similar creature called the "bouncer" (Uw'tsûñ'ta) lived on the Nantahala River in North Carolina. It too moved by "jerks like a measuring worm." According to lore this snake like animal was so immense that it would darken the valleys between rifts as it moved across them. According to Mooney the Indians that lived in this area, fearing the snake eventually deserted the land, "even while still Indian country." [224]

Another monstrous snake, called the Uktena, was said to be as large as a tree trunk with horns on its head. Anyone skillful enough to kill the Uktena would obtain a transparent scale from the snake, said to be similar to a crystal that was located on its forehead. To have such a scale was a blessing which would bring excellent hunting, success in love, rainmaking and life prophecy.

Some Native American people viewed the snake in another way entirely. It was symbolic of the war-god who also had powers over crops and vegetation. "As the emblem of the fertilizing summer showers the lightning serpent was the god of fruitfulness," wrote Lewis Spence, "but as the forerunner of floods and disastrous rains it was feared and dreaded." [225]

---

[223] Mooney, op cit 1995, 302.
[224] Ibid, 304.
[225] Spence, Lewis. *North American Indians Myths & Legends.* London: Senate 1994, 112. A reprint of *North American Indians* published 1914 by George G. Harrap & Company Ltd.

That prehistoric Indians believed the serpent form contained supernatural powers can be surmised by the various serpent mounds constructed in the American heartland. Three such mounds are those found in Adams County, Ohio, St. Peter's River, Iowa and another serpentine mound which extends in sections over two miles in length, also in Iowa. The Great Serpent Mound located in Adams County, Ohio is believed to be the largest serpent effigy in the world at over one-quarter of a mile in length and depicts a serpent in the act of uncoiling. [226] This unusual earthwork shows the serpent with an egg, perhaps the Cosmic Egg, in its mouth. The culture that created the Great Serpent Mound is unknown since no manmade artifact has been found in connection with the site, although Adena artifacts consisting of copper breastplates, stone points and axes, and grooved sandstone have been found within 400 feet of the mound.

American folklore has a number of superstitions surrounding the snake. Among these is the notion that a snake cannot cross a horsehair rope but that horsehair placed in a bucket of water will turn into a snake. "A spotted serpent called the milk snake," reports folklorist Vance Randolph, "is said to live by milking cows in the pasture. I know several persons who swear they have seen these snakes sucking milk cows, and they say that a cow which has been milked by a snake is always reluctant to allow a human being to touch her thereafter." [227]

---

[226] Silverberg, Robert. *Mound Builders of Ancient America: The Archaeology of a Myth.* Greenwich: New York Graphic Society Ltd. 1968, 249.
[227] Randolph, Vance. *Ozark Magic and Folklore.* New York: Dover Publications, Inc. 1964, 257. A reprint of the 1947 edition of *Ozark Superstitions* published by Columbia University Press.

South West American Indian petroglyph of the snake with the cosmic egg.

While the snake was often feared, American "hill folk" also respected it. According to Randolph, rather than say the word "snake," like the Apache, "they say 'look out for *our friends* down that way,' or 'there's a lot of *them old things* between here and the river.'" [228]

British folklore says, "if you wear a snake skin round your head, you will never have a headache" and "snakes never die until the sun goes down, however much they may be cut in pieces." [229] However, "if you kill one its mate will come

---

[228] Ibid, 258.
[229] Radford, Edwin and Mona A. *Encyclopaedia of Superstitions.* New York: Philosophical Library 1949, 221.

looking for you." [230]Another advises that to stay young—eat snake!

In 19th century Gaelic folklore the serpent is more evil than good. Campbell wrote, "A serpent, whenever encountered, ought to be killed. Otherwise, the encounter will prove an evil omen.

"The head should be completely smashed...and removed to a distance from the rest of the body. Unless this is done the serpent will again come alive. The tail, unless deprived of animation, will join the body, and the head becomes a *beithir*, the largest and most deadly kind of serpent." [231]

In other cultures, like many Native American ones, there is a prohibition against killing snakes. Frazer wrote "In Madras it is considered a great sin to kill a cobra. When this has happened, the people generally burn the body of the serpent, just as they burn the bodies of human beings. The murderer deems himself polluted for three days."[232] In other areas of the world, snakes were annually sacrificed in large numbers by burning. This occurred at Luchon in the Pyrenees on Midsummer Eve at least into the early 20th century. Considered a Pagan survival, the ritual was led by the local clergy. Frazer describes the event:

"At an appointed hour—about 8 PM—a grand procession, composed of the clergy, followed by young men and maidens in holiday attire, pour forth from the town chanting hymns, and take up their position [around a wicker-work column raised 60 feet in height]. ...bonfires are lit, with beautiful effect, in the surrounding hills. As many living serpents as

---

[230] Simpson, Jacqueline and Steve Roud. *Oxford Dictionary of English Folklore*. Oxford: Oxford University Press 2000, 2.
[231] Campbell, John Gregorson. *The Gaelic Otherworld*, edited by Ronald Black. Edinburgh: Birlinn Limited 2005, 121.
[232] Frazer, Sir James. *The Golden Bough: A study in magic and religion*. Hertfordshire: Wordsworth Editions 1993, 222.

could be collected are now thrown into the column, which is set on fire at the base by means of torches, armed with which about fifty boys and men dance around with frantic gestures. The serpents…wriggle their way to the top…until finally obliged to drop, their struggles for life giving rise to enthusiastic delight among the surrounding spectators." [233]

Serpents have been mercilessly hunted and killed by many cultures the world over but it is possible, according to Jyoti Sahi, that "all religions which have evolved the concept of a really personal god…have emerged out of a tradition in which serpents have been extremely important symbols of the supernatural." [234]

Snakes with horns? They are common in Celtic crafts and mythology and represent protection against all forms of catastrophe — sickness, war and all of the horrors of death. According to Miranda Green, approximately fifteen examples of horned serpents can be found in Gaul while only a handful more are seen throughout the British Isles. [235]

The ram horned serpent almost always appears as a companion to Celtic deities such as Cernunnos, who himself is stag-horned. This monstrous snake appears on the Gundestrup Cauldron on one panel with Cernunnos and on another at the head of a military march. Miranda Green noted that the ram horned snake appears on a carving at Haute Marne accompanying a goddess who feeds the snake from a basket on her knee and at Loire on a wooden sculpture with a possible Cernunnos figure. The serpent slides down the god's arm with its head in a basket. "The repeated prosperity-symbolism," Green writes "shown in reliefs is significant: a

---

[233] Ibid 655-656.
[234] Sahi, op cit 166.
[235] Green, Miranda. *The Gods of the Celts*. Gloucester: Alan Sutton 1986, 192.

bronze from...Seine et Loire combines several Celtic images in curious intensity; a three-headed god sits cross-legged...[with] a ram-horned snake entwined round his body."[236]

The horned snake was also an important religious image in other areas of the world. As noted previously, the Mesopotamian god Ningiszida was depicted as a horned snake, appearing on such items as ritual cups and city seals. Images of horned snakes were commonly used in the Mesopotamian world as magically protective charms.

In Mexico, Central and South America it is the jaguar rather than the snake that is important in the indigenous religious traditions.

Aztec shamans wore the hides, including the snout, hearts, claws, tails, and fangs, of jaguars and were said to be greatly feared because of the powers these objects transferred to the shaman. [237]

"In a tropical jungle where every rustle in the undergrowth, every cracking twig may betray the presence of a big cat, a belief in jaguar gods or spirits is only natural," wrote Walter Krickeberg. [238] The likeness of the jaguar was often carved into valuable jade, quartz and basalt religious objects used ceremonially or as offerings.

Large altars and lithic carvings were crafted as representative of the jaguar body and face, often as gaping jaws which symbolized both the heavens and the underworld.

Some believe that the jaguar was the totem animal of "the corpulent people" who were the lower caste while the "thinner people" who were the ruling class and the builders

---

[236] Ibid.
[237] Miller, Mary and Karl Taube. *An Illustrated Dictionary of The Gods and Symbols of Ancient Mexico and the Maya.* London: Thames and Hudson Ltd., 1993, 102.
[238] Krickeberg, op cit., 11.

of the great monuments valued the serpent.[239] This theory is unlikely however in regards to thin or fat people but it could be correct that these particular totem animals were valued by different classes of people.

Realistic clay figures of jaguars were important ritual pieces in Mayan culture and attest to the importance of the animal if their cosmological view.

Reproduction of a Mayan jaguar figure.

---

[239] Ibid., 13.

V
Native American Use of Amulets

The use of amulets and charms, both as physical items and for invocation and chants, is well known in Native American tribal culture. As wandering hunters and gatherers, it was very important for the Native American to have some communication and influence with deities, spirits and totems so that the basic necessities of life could be satisfied. For the most part the Native American shaman was the keeper of charms and amulets but the individual may also have possessed certain items to provide luck, protection and success in hunting and fishing. An example of such an amulet is shown in the photograph on the next page. In this case, a bear tooth had been strung on a necklace by a Woodland Indian several hundred years ago and worn as a symbol not only of bravery but possibly used to provide protection and success in the hunt. These items were often thought to provide a communications link with the gods or the spirits of animals.

Nineteenth century anthropologist James Mooney recorded his interview with John Wilson, one of the participants in the Ghost Dance religion. Wilson possessed an amulet that Mooney found of interest:

...on his breast, suspended from a cord about his neck, was a curious amulet consisting of the polished end of a buffalo horn, surrounded by a circlet of downy red feathers, within another circle of badger and owl claws. He explained that this was the source of his prophetic and clairvoyant inspiration. The buffalo horn was 'God's heart,' the red feathers contained his own heart, and the circle of claws represented the world. When he prayed for help, his heart communed with 'God's heart,' and he learned what he wished to know. [240]

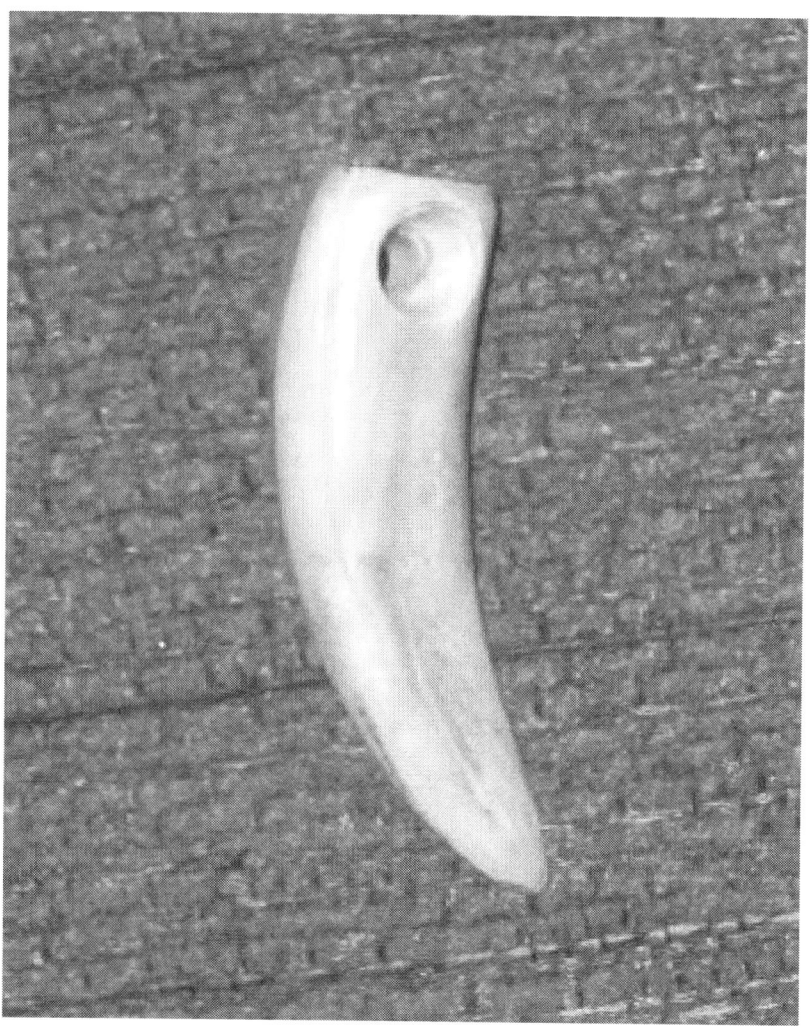

The inherent magical properties of unusual items such as the buffalo horn were believed to offer luck and protection

---

[240] Mooney, James. *The Ghost Dance Religion and the Sioux Outbreak of 1890.* Chicago: University of Chicago Press 1965, 161-162.

against adversity, trouble with evil, or health issues. Many of the amulets used by people are natural objects with unnatural shapes and/or color. The photo of the stone shown below is one such example.

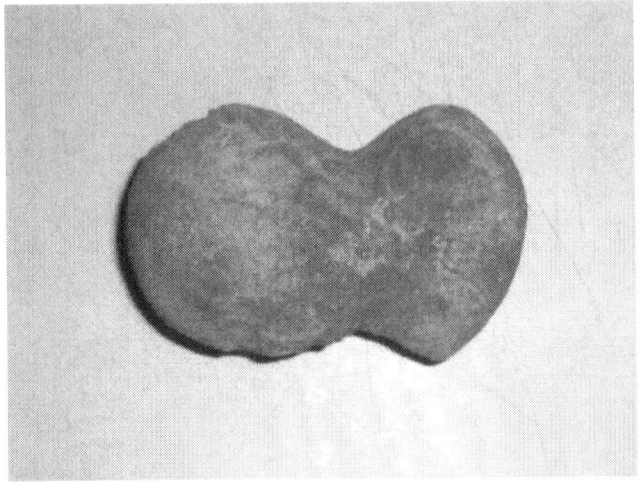

Others have a more direct link with gods and goddesses. Figurines, carved from stone or fashioned from clay and most often female in nature, are found in many archaeological excavations. Many times they represent ancestors or goddesses, fertility or some aspect of nature. They also act as amulets. The photo on the next page shows five figurines found at the ancient Sinagua Indian site of Tuzigoot in the Verde Valley of Arizona. These figurines were actually "planted" in the soil to ensure an abundance of corn and other crops that were heavily relied on. In this way, these figurines were prized amulets, important to the very existence of the Sinaguans. They were used by the Sinagua people prior to their disappearance from the area around 1400 CE.

Similar figurines were made by the Hohokam people as well. Archaeologists believe that these figurines, such as the Hohokam and the Tuzigoot figures, "is related to that of

Mexico" and "are usually related, as they are around the world, to fertility." [241]

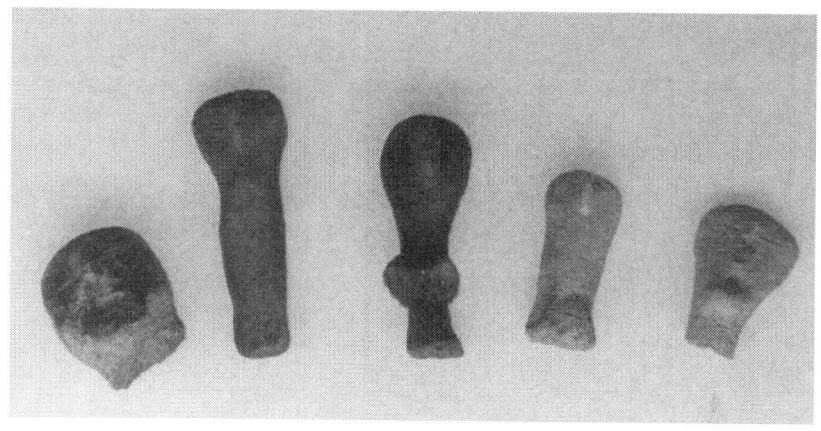

Tuzigoot fertility amulets, Arizona.

Unusual natural objects were widely venerated by Native American and other indigenous people around the world. "Among the Onas," wrote John Cooper in his 1916 account of this South American tribe, "there is a marked tendency to look upon natural objects as having once been men. "The Yahgans carried around with them red pebbles when they traveled inland...and the Onas treasure pieces of stone shaped naturally something like an arrowhead..." [242]

The Apache were fond of wearing amulets carved from "lightning-riven wood," generally pine, cedar or fir gathered in the mountains. "These are shaved very thin and rudely cut

---

[241] Gumerman, George J. and Emil W. Haury. "Prehistory: Hohokam" in *Handbook of North American Indians, Volume 9: Southwest.* Washington: Smithsonian Institution 1979, 79.

[242] Cooper, John M. *Analytical and Critical Bibliography of the Tribes of Tierra del Fuego and Adjacent Territory.* Bureau of American Ethnology Bulletin 63. Washington: Smithsonian Institution 1917, 150.

in the semblance of the human form," wrote 19th century ethnologist John G. Bourke. [243]

According to Bourke these wooden figures were attached to the cradle boards of children or the child wore them around his neck. These amulets had significant powers, as Bourke related:

> The owner of this inestimable treasure assured me that he prayed to it at all times when in trouble, that he could learn from it where his ponies were when stolen and which was the right direction to travel when lost, and that when drought had parched his crops this would never fail to bring rain in abundance to revive and strengthen them. [244]

Numerous other amulets were used as well by the Apache, including many used for the protection of children. Morris Edward Opler who studied the Chiricahua Apache in the 1930s noted:

To the amulets and pendants supplied by the shaman the mother generally adds some of her own. The right paw of the badger, with grass substituted for the bone, is hung on the cradle to guard the child from fright. Such protection is important, for fright lies at the root of a number of serious illnesses. Humming bird claws and pieces of wildcat skin also act as cradle charms. [245]

The Apache shaman also carried turquoise which Bourke referred to as "impure malachite." "A small bead of this mineral," he reported, "affixed to a gun or bow made the

---

[243] Bourke, John G. *Apache Medicine-Men.* New York: Dover Publications, Inc. 1993, 137.
[244] Ibid.
[245] Opler, Morris Edward. *An Apache Life-Way: The Economic, Social, and Religious Institutions of the Chirichaua Indians.* Chicago: University of Chicago Press 1941, 12.

weapon shoot accurately. It had also some relation to the bringing of rain...It was the Apache medicine-man's badge of office...and without it he could not in olden times exercise his medical functions." [246]

Apache tradition stated that turquoise could only be found if one traveled to the end of a rainbow after a storm and searched in the damp earth at that spot. Perhaps the story of finding a pot of gold at the end of a rainbow originated in this Native American tradition.

Bear amulets have been found in North Britain and other areas and, as they were in North America, have been found in burials. A small child was found buried near Malton in Yorkshire with a tiny black bear-amulet [247] showing perhaps the belief that the bear helped the soul on its way to the underworld.

Zuni animal totem, 19th century. Photograph courtesy Carnegie Museum of Natural History, Pittsburgh, Pennsylvania.

---

[246] Bourke, op cit., 139.
[247] Green, Miranda. *The Gods of the Celts*. Glouchester: Alan Sutton 1986, 184.

Indian craftsmen in the Southwest were responsible for many beautiful ritual and amuletic objects, including carvings of snakes, toads, and birds. Their techniques included acid etching on shells, pottery, lost wax molds and stone art. One of the most simple but striking amulet I have seen is the split-twig animal figurine of a deer found in a cave overlooking Marble Canyon in Arizona. It was found hidden in a rockshelter and is believed to have been used for sympathetic hunting magic.

Among the South and Central American Indians the jaguar was the power of darkness and the messenger of the forest spirits. It was also a form taken by shape-shifting shamans in their quest for union with the gods.

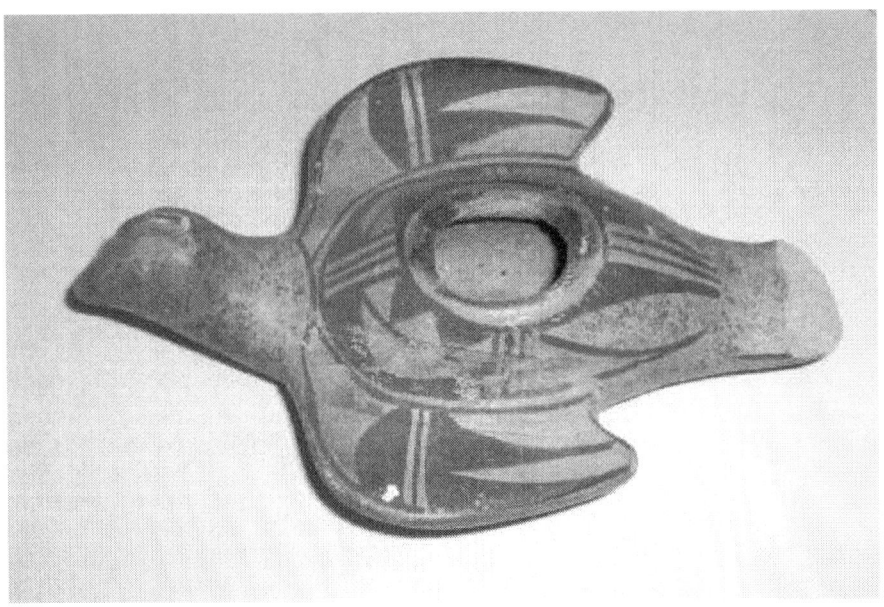

A Southwest Native American vessel probably used by shamans to burn sage or other incense.

VI
Charms

Other forms of ancient charms and amulets, tools used to affect a curse, are the small human form figures commonly referred to today as voodoo dolls. Originally known as *kolossi* in Greek, they are not nearly as common as lead tablets but they are far older. Made of lead, wax, bronze, clay, mud, and dough, these dolls have been dated to the 10th century BCE. Actual voodoo dolls have been found from the Imperial Rome era in a riverbed and a sewer. It is believed that the use of voodoo dolls in Imperial Rome began at around the same time curse tablets were being used.

In antiquity, acts of magic, including spell-craft through incantation, were not considered as any form of opposition to the established religion. Ancient Rome's law code, called the *Twelve Tables*, only prohibits evil incantations—not beneficial spell-craft. Scholar Marie-Louis Thomsen wrote, "They were not regarded as superstitious or forbidden, or laughed at. The rituals called 'magical' were the ordinary way of dealing with illness and misfortune and whatever disturbed the relations between man and god. In the eyes of the Mesopotamians they represented an old and divine knowledge and their performers were learned men with a high social status." [248]

A sorcerer may yield tremendous power by using his or her ability to make others ill to the point of death. Such ability may be used intentionally or unintentionally but will result in the same end. Anthropologist Beatrice Blyth Whiting, who studied Paiute sorcery, noted in her 1950 study, "When a sorcerer is angry, he may unintentionally kill someone in one

---

[248] Thomsen, Marie-Louise. "Witchcraft and Magic in Ancient Mesopotamia" in *Witchcraft and Magic in Europe: Biblical and Pagan Societies.* Philadelphia: University of Pennsylvania Press 2001, 14.

of the following ways: he may think bad thoughts about the individual without being aware of his thoughts; in a fit of temper he may express aggressive wishes about an individual without the intention of injuring him; or he may dream bad dreams about an individual. In the latter case, the victim may have dreams in which the sorcerer's power appears."[249]

Many individuals appear to have been accused of witchcraft due to personality defects more than anything else. One example recorded by Whiting was in the case of a man named Tom who lived near Fort Bidwell in Oregon in the 1930s. Tom was regarded as "mean"; he supposedly beat his children for little reason, was said to be "aggressive in competitive games and was domineering and threatening in his relationship with other tribal members. Naturally, he was accused of witchcraft because of his lack of control and disregard for societal norms. [250]

Anyone who exhibited similar characteristics during the Middle Ages was also regarded as a witch or sorcerer. Such charges were a way to enforce cultural norms in behavior and group cooperation.

There are, of course, instances where people have and do desire to create harm and use many of the typical methods of witchcraft to achieve their goal — through spell-craft.

Perhaps one of the oldest forms of spell-craft using incantations is that of "metrical charms" — simple rhymes that have carried over into contemporary cultures as nursery rhymes.

The power of language, of particular words and sounds, has long been valued by cultures which have not invested their entire experience in obtaining knowledge through the

---

[249] Whiting, Beatrice Blyth. *Paiute Sorcery: Viking Fund Publications in Anthropology Number Fifteen.* New York: The Viking Fund 1950, 56.
[250] Ibid. 61.

written word. While I cannot think of a world without books, it is, sad to say, the written language which has robbed modern man of his ability to utilize his mind as once was done.

Caesar reported that the Druids underwent 20 years of intense education. A huge number of verses and oral history was required to be mastered before an initiate could pass the Druidic training. None of the required training could be committed to writing. Likewise Australian aborigine societies continue to educate their young in a similar fashion, as did Native Americans at one time.

Incantations by verse were perhaps the first form of spell-craft. Spence reports one such spell used to bind an individual to a particular task. Called the "nine fulfillments of the fairy woman" it ran as follows:

> To lay thee under spells and crosses
> under (pain of being struck by) the nine
>   cow-fetters of the wildly roaming,
>   traveler-deluding fairy woman,
> So that some sorry little wight more feeble
>   and misguided than myself
> Take thy head, thine ear and thy life's
> career from thee. [251]

Another example of a spell called a *fath-fifth* or *fith-fath* which supposedly causes invisibility is, according to Spense:

> A magic cloud I put on thee,
> From dog, from cat,
> From cow, from horse,

---

[251] Spence, Lewis. *The Magic Arts in Celtic Britain.* Mineola: Dover Publications, Inc. 1999, 62.

From man, from woman,
From young man, from maiden,
And from little child.
Till I again return. [252]

16th century illustration of witches and sorcerers.

The term *fith-fath*, pronounced "fee-fa" survived in our nursery rhymes as the giant's chant "fee-fo-fum" in Jack and the Beanstalk.

Another example of an incantation is found in Shakespeare's Macbeth:

"Double double, toil and trouble…"

Other rhyming incantations were said to be used to transform a witch into an animal, in this example it was used to shape-shift into a hare:

---

[252] Ibid., 60.

> I shall go into a hare,
> With sorrow and sigh and mickle care;
> And I shall go in the Devil's name
> Ay while I come home again.

As previously noted, the Roman *Twelve Tables* only prohibited spells used to harm others, not those used for the good of society. Fritz Graf, professor of classics at Princeton University, sums up the intent of the *Twelve Tables*:
"The Romans evidently believed in the powerful efficacy of certain vocal rites, the *carmina*, one could *incantare* or *excantare*. But we do not know whether the negative value of these terms is peculiar to them or whether it comes from the context…The same law of the Twelve Tables also uses *Carmen* in the neutral sense of verbal composition, according to Cicero: 'If any person had sung or composed against another person a song such as was causing slander or insult to another…' As defamatory songs, these *carmina* also have a destructive force…" [253]

The use of sound to control weather, or at least to cause rain, was practiced in the Ozarks in the United States up to the early part of the 20th century. According to Vance Randolph "Singing late at night is said to 'fetch on a shower,' as explained in the little rhyme:

> Sing afore you go to bed,
> You'll get up with a wet head." [254]

---

[253] Graf, Fritz. *Magic in the Ancient World.* Cambridge: Harvard University Press 1997, 42.
[254] Randolph, Vance. *Ozark Magic and Folklore.* New York: Dover Publications, Inc. 1964, 31.

The History & Use of Amulets, Charms and Talismans

Egypt has had a long history of using magical incantations. Some of the oldest and most complete magical texts still in existence date to the first century BCE. Magical names and characters were common but also the simple use of long magical words repeated over and over.

Religion historian Richard Kieckhefer wrote "papyri sometimes repeat long magical words, progressively abridged with each repetition, such as:

ablanathanablanamacharamacharamarach
ablanathanablanamacharamacharamara
ablanathanablanamacharamacharamar

"And so forth, until nothing but the initial 'A' remains." [255] At the same time, Kieckhefer noted, "magicians in the Mediterranean world were devising other magical words like 'abracadabra' and 'abraxas' to use on amulets or papyri." [256]

"Abracadabra" is a widespread incantation normally used today in cartoons or by persons not knowing its significance that, according to Mare Köiva, "has gradually taken on the meaning on the unknown and the unintelligible." [257]

"Abraxas" is an interesting word supposedly derived from "the holy name of God." The sum of the seven letters equals 365 or the number of days in a year. [258]

The use of "magical words" became very popular during the Middle Ages and have been linked to cabalistic texts. Many of the written incantations were accompanied with graphic designs such as circles, squares, crosses, images of the

---

[255] Kieckhefer, op cit, 20.
[256] Ibid.
[257] Köiva, Mare. "Palindromes and Letter Formulae: Some Reconsiderations" in *Folklore*, Vol. 8, December 1998. Published by the Institute of Estonian Language, Tartu, 21.
[258] Ibid., 29.

sun, etc. These magic words were often arranged in circles or squares, called palindromes, in which each letter and word may have specific meanings. During the Middle Ages they were utilized by the Muslims and cabalists but have been found in Coptic scrolls as well.

Köiva notes "In the 18ths century at the apogee of the use of the formula (in Estonia), the incantation was attached to planks, clay tablets or plates that were put up on the walls of houses or outhouses. At times of war and extensive fires such incantations were burnt in order to prevent fire." [259]

This formula was used in Estonia for protection from fire, rabies, snakebite, swelling, toothache, bleeding and to ensure successful hunting ventures.

Like the early Greeks and Romans, the early Christians also tolerated, if not embraced, neutral or beneficial magic. The difficulty, as Kieckhefer relates, "was in telling whether a particular practice did or did not involve appeal to demons."[260] Demonic magic was never tolerated in Christian or, for that matter, in any other society. "One of the most common tests," Kieckhefer continues, "was whether [a particular practice]…contained unintelligible words that might in fact be names for demons." [261]

While charms and spell-craft were considered "heathen" practices ("heathen" a term applied to those living in uncultivated, wild and forested lands—in other words, "peasants") it was not entirely so. James Scott, the Duke of Monmouth, illegitimate son of King Charles II and pretender to the British throne, was arrested in the early 1680s and

---

[259] Ibid., 23.
[260] Ibid.,182.
[261] Ibid.

banished from the country. [262] On his arrest, a "pocket-book" of handwritten "spells, charms, and conjurations, songs, receipts, and prayers" [263] was recovered.

Among the items contained in the book were "magical receipts and charms in French, written partly in abbreviated form, accompanied by cabalistic figures. Two of these are to deliver a person out of prison..." [264]

The book also contained incantations to turn gray hair black, protection against violent death and deliverance from "pains."

In many areas of the world, magic and spell-casting is still a very important function in survival. The Qemant, an ethnic Pagan-Hebraic group that lived in Ethiopia prior to the civil war there, practiced "white" magic to counteract the power of malevolent magic and witchcraft. According to anthropologist Frederick Gamst who studied the Qemant, "magic is practiced by all shamans, by certain knowledgeable peasants of any ethnic group, and by some religious practitioners of the Christian and Muslim faiths." [265]

Qemant sorcerers, who practice black magic, rely on incantations and "objects of medicine" for their spells. All of this may be counteracted by the shaman who practices "white magic" using primarily the same methods.

---

[262] He returned to England later in an attempt to take the crown by force but was defeated and executed for treason in 1685 by John Churchill, 1st Duke of Marlborough.
[263] Madden, Sir F. "The Duke of Monmouth's Pocket-books" in *Notes and Queries*, Vol. IV, No. 88, Saturday, July 5, 1851, 2.
[264] Ibid.
[265] Gamst, Frederick C. *The Qemant: A Pagan-Hebraic Peasantry of Ethiopia.* New York: Holt, Rinehart and Winston Case Studies in Cultural Anthopology 1969, 54.

VII
Stones as Amulets and Charms

The supernatural powers believed to be inherent in stones have caused them to be used as charms for thousands of years. They were worn to protect against the anger of certain gods, to profit in business transactions, to keep diseases and evil at bay, to heal and to gather the energy needed to acquire abundance. It was a common practice in Great Britain to scrape dust and particles from ancient stones, including Stonehenge, and mix the dust with water to drink as a remedy for various illnesses. While we usually think of amulets and charms as small, portable objects, this is not always the case. Standing stones weighing several tons have been utilized as powerful amulets over time.

Charmed stones were used by the mightiest of rulers to the commonest of the common. Two fourteen-stone chains have been attributed to Naram-Sin, a famous conqueror and ruler of the Akkadian Empire, and to the king of Babylon and lawgiver Hammurabi. These two chains were composed of lapis lazuli, green obsidian and jasper. [266] While the purpose of the chains is not known, it is believed that they were considered to possess powers to enhance the abilities of the two kings to rule.

The Pima Indians who lived between the Santa Cruz and San Pablo Rivers, in Arizona, reportedly used stone tablets, which they had found in ruins left by earlier peoples, in healing rituals. Frustratingly little information remains to

---

[266] Thomsen, Marie-Louise. "Witchcraft and Magic in Ancient Mesopotamia," in *Witchcraft and Magic in Europe: Biblical and Pagan Societies.* Edited by Bengt Ankarloo and Stuart Clark. Philadelphia: University of Pennsylvania Press, 2001, 60.

suggest where these tablets came from or how they were used. [267] Other stone tablets have been found in many of the Adena mounds in American Midwest — some of which supposedly have Roman and Arabic figures or letters similar to Phoenician characters. Researchers have theorized that the true purpose of these tablets was to stamp cult designs on bodies being buried or newly initiated members of the tribe or for stamping designs on textiles. [268] They also may represent religious items of an unknown purpose.

The belief in the magical protective powers of stones continues, among some people, into the present day. The Iraqi dictator Saddam Hussein, captured by American forces in December 2003, was reportedly protected by a magical stone. Iraqi lore says that Hussein once placed the stone on the back of a cow, fired a shot at the cow, and watched as the bullet swerved around the animal, leaving it unscathed. [269] While many Americans scoff at such beliefs, none can dispute the fact that he survived several attempts by American forces to kill him with "bunker busters" and suffered only a bump on his head when captured. It didn't seem to protect him from the hangman's noose, however.

Many odd beliefs have survived into modern times, despite all society's effort to introduce science and rationalism. In Utah, at least through the 1950s, wearing pale blue stones around the neck was believed to relieve headaches. Some also believed that these stones could prevent or stop bleeding. It was a practice in the Ozark Mountains (in Missouri and Arkansas), at least until the 1920s, to sew small

---

[267] Spier, Leslie. *Yuman Tribes of the Gila River.* New York: Dover Publications Inc., 1978, 283 (originally published 1933).
[268] Silverberg, Robert. *Mound Builders of Ancient America: The Archaeology of a Myth.* Greenwich: New York Graphic Society Ltd., 1968, 249.
[269] Hider, James. "Even on the run, Hussein has Iraqis under his 'spell,'" in *The Christian Science Monitor*, August 6, 2003.

stones into children's clothes to protect them from common childhood diseases.

In various locations throughout the world, the "evil eye" was warded off by taking stones found on river and creek banks, drilling holes in them, and placing them on strings around the neck of children. Amber was worn around the neck in many areas of the world including Spain, Kentucky, Utah, Illinois, Ohio and the Pacific Southwest as a protection against heart disease and as an aid in curing such physical ailments as colds, flu, convulsions, goiter, whooping cough, teething, lung ailments, sore throat, poisons, eye ailments, neck swelling and to prevent sexual desire. Necklaces of chalcedony (a broad class of mineral that includes carnelian, agate and jasper) were worn around the neck to ward off or bring recovery from insanity.

The belief that certain stones hold supernatural powers seems to date back to the Stone Age. A belief in the transference of diseases or evil to stones, or, through stones to other persons, is found in ethnological and folklore accounts worldwide. At one time, it was customary for people living in the Indonesian Babar Archipelago to strike themselves with stones and throw them away, in the belief that they could transfer their fatigue to the stones.

Stones of different types were used universally to combat illness. Fever was believed to be transferable to agate — place an agate on the individual's head and the fever would move to the stone, and leave the patient relieved. A Scottish treatment for fever states that the person should hold three stones from a streambed in his hands and mouth while quietly lying down. Lewis Spence noted in his book, *The Magic Arts in Celtic Britain*, "the number of miraculous stones existing, or formerly existing, in Scotland and Ireland 'defies description.'"

Infertility has always been one of the most troubling conditions that can befall a family — there is mystery in its cause, and certainly a mystery in how it might be overcome. Stones were often looked to for help. In Burgos, Spain, a fountain dedicated to Saint Casilda was reported to have the power to make a woman fertile; and if a stone was thrown into the waters, a baby boy was assured. If a girl was desired, then tiles were tossed into the fountain. In Armenia, it is said that barren women would visit the rocky cleft in the mountain pass at Varanta. Legends said that if she was to have a child, the stone would open wide enough to let her pass, but she would not get through if she was not going to have a baby. [270]

Near the Scottish village of Ratho, seven miles from Edinburgh, women used the Witch's Stone, a large sloping boulder (now destroyed) with ancient marks cut into it, to encourage fertility; they would slide down the stone, in the belief that this would assist them in conceiving. A similar stone used in the same way is located in Kings Park, Edinburgh. The stones were highly polished by the many women who had slid down them over the years.

A similar tradition was practiced across the English Channel, in Brittany, where, according to Michell, "the grand menhir brisé was not just a possible lunar foresight but an actual resort, annually on the first of May, for women in search of offspring, which they hoped to achieve by bare-arsed slidings along its fragments." [271]

The obelisk of Begig, located southwest of Madînat al-Fayyûm Egypt, was also popular place of visitation for barren women. Women wishing children believed that by touching

---

[270] Lalayan, E. "Veranda: Family Customs," in *Ethnographic Review* #2 (1897), 186.
[271] Michell, John. *Megalithomania*. Ithaca: Cornell University Press, 1982, 89.

the obelisk, it would ensure their ability to bear strong and healthy children.

This practice was also part of California Indian tradition. A large "fertility stone" in an ancient Maidu village located in present day Roseville, California has carvings of breasts and a vulva which the Maidu girls would rub to ensure their fertility. These massive fertility stones were believed to house the spirits of ancestors, who would help the girl become pregnant. In some cultures, these spirits would impregnate the girl so that the spirit could be reborn once again. Similar legends occur in Sioux lore, wherein the mother of Stone Boy (a Lakotah cultural hero said to have been "miraculously born") swallows a pebble and becomes pregnant, and in the Aztec myth of the birth of the god Quetzalcoatl. Interestingly, folk notions regarding humankind's origin from stone appear to be repeated in stories about the origin of the gods, themselves. According to legend, Chimalma, while she was sweeping one day, found a piece of jade and swallowed it — and became pregnant, giving birth to Quetzalcoatl, as a result. "The Mexicans," wrote 19th-century US Cavalry officer John G. Bourke, "were accustomed to say that at one time all men have been stones, and at last they would all return to stones," upon death. [272] Similar beliefs have been recorded in Oceania where it was said that rocks gave birth to all things in the world. In Africa, according to John Mbiti, "the Akamba have a rock in the western central part of their country, at Nzaui, which has a hole supposed to be the one through which God brought out the first man and wife."[273]

---

[272] Bourke, John G. *Apache Medicine-Men.* New York: Dover Publications, Inc., 1993, 141.
[273] Mbiti, John S. *African Religions and Philosophy.* Garden City: Anchor Books 1970, 121

Archaeologist Campbell Grant wrote, "in many parts of the West, isolated boulders are covered with the distinctive pit-and-groove markings. Such carved boulders are especially abundant in northern California, and in the Pomo territory were known as 'baby rocks' and were used ceremonially by women wanting children." [274] McGowan notes that these rocks in the Pomo territory were frequented by childless couples, who would "grind off a bit of the rock in one of the cupules and make a paste of the dust. A design was drawn on the abdomen of the woman and some of the paste inserted into her vagina. Intercourse at this time ensured that she would become pregnant." [275]

The Kawaiisu Indians of California's Great Basin area also frequented a special rock to ensure fertility. The three foot tall standing stone, known as "one who is a little pregnant." due to its shape, was visited by women seeking to bear children. Kawaiisu women would break off small pieces of the rock and swallow them, believing that the stone chips would impregnate them.

A fertility amulet, also known as a pregnancy stone, was commonly used in Italy. As Walton McDaniel recorded in 1948 in the *Journal of the History of Medicine*:

> [The amulet was] in the shape of a womb…a limonitic concretion or brown hematite, which, on being shaken, produces a sound…the prospective mother wears it nine months, fastened to the right arm, but then, at the arrival of the first pains of partition, she transfers it to the right thigh. Women

---

[274] Grant, Campbell. *Rock Art of the American Indian.* New York: Promontory Press, 1967, 31.
[275] McGowan, Charlotte. *Ceremonial Fertility Sites in Southern California: San Diego Museum of Man Papers No. 14.* San Diego: San Diego Museum of Man, 1982, 14.

hire the use of these stones from a midwife, if they do not possess one of their own as a family heirloom. Although these amuletic objects might seem to be somewhat pagan, grateful mothers do not hesitate to deposit them as tokens of success, as ex-votos in a Christian Church. [276]

A folktale of the Yupa Indians of Venezuela speaks of a Yupa woman who "found a stone from which she made a phallus. By having relations with this stone she finally got herself with child and bore a daughter." [277] Women in New Zealand would visit a boulder at Kawhia, called Uenuku-tuwhartu. The boulder was credited with having the power to cure infertility. One side of the boulder was regarded as the male side and the other the female side; the woman would clasp one side or the other, depending on the desired gender of the hoped-for child.

Certain standing stones in Hawaii and Fiji, from six to eight feet in height, were regarded as having phallic powers and thus became fertility shrines. Andersen writes that two such pillars near Puna, Hawaii, had been used in ritual ceremonies since the earliest occupation of the islands. Those in Fiji, according to early ethnologists, were regarded as "consecrated stones" and were periodically given offerings of food. These were described "as like a round black milestone, slightly inclined, with a liku tied around the middle. The liku is a band with a close-set fringe…and its presence accentuates the phallic character of the stone." [278]

---

[276] McDaniel, Walton Brooks. "The Medical and Magical Significance in Ancient Medicine of Things Connected with Reproduction and Its Organs," in *Journal of the History of Medicine, 3 (1948)*, page 543.

[277] Wilbert, Johannes. *Yupa Folktales*. Los Angeles: Latin American Center, University of Los Angeles, 1974, 92.

[278] Andersen, Johannes C. *Myths and Legends of the Polynesians*. Rutland: Charles E. Tuttle Company, 1969, 413.

In some areas around the world, difficulties in childbirth were avoided by wearing, or keeping close, stones the color of the sea, such as beryl. Stones with holes in them were especially prized and it was believed that suspending one over a woman in labor would give her a much easier childbirth and protect mother and infant against evil. In Roman times, it was believed that a stone used to kill a powerful animal (or a strong man) also had the power to make childbirth easier. The stone was thrown over the house where the woman lay in labor. [279]

For those worried about the inability to conceive, one possible solution was to collect stones from the property of couples who had many children; bringing such stones to one's own household was thought to bring fertility with them. This belief was still present in 1950s Arkansas. [280] In ancient Egypt, it was a practice to make scratch marks on stones in the belief that by doing so, pregnancy would be induced. [281] Other stones were used in Greece, Albania and Germany to ensure that the mother would have an abundant supply of milk for the baby.

Conversely, rock crystal was used by the Apache Indians attempting to prevent pregnancy. According to ethnologist Morris Opler, "rock crystal is used as a medicine when a woman does not want a child. The rock is ground up fine, and some of the powder is put in a drink. There are prayers and a ceremony connected with this, but I do not know them." [282] Bourke notes that a "medicine arrow" worn as an amulet by

---

[279] De Lys, Claudia. *A Treasury of American Superstitions*. New York: The Philosophical Library, 1948, 216.
[280] Parler, Mary Celestia. *Folk Beliefs from Arkansas, Vol 3*. Fayetteville: University of Arkansas, 1962, 9.
[281] Leland, Charles G. "Marks on Ancient Monuments" in *Folk-Lore*, 8 (1897), page 86.
[282] Lalayan. *op. cit.*, 186.

Apache medicine-women was broken or ground into fine powder and given to women during gestation. Whether to aid the pregnancy or to abort it, he does not say. [283] The medicine arrow was reportedly taken from the top of a mountain at the foot of a tree that had been struck by lightning.

Ethnographic evidence indicates that Comanche shamans used stones at least into the 1970s, if not later, in healing rituals. Ethnologist David E. Jones wrote that a medicine woman he had studied "applied the stone peyote drum 'bosses' to the patient's face so that, through her powers, the positive qualities of these stones — firmness and stability — could be injected into the patient's contorted face to heal him." [284]

Shiva's Lingam Stones

The Indian god Shiva is represented in sacred stones taken from the River Narmada, in central-western India. The Narmada is one of the seven sacred Hindu sites of pilgrimage in India. Believed to be the most sacred icon of ancient and modern India, these particular stones, ranging in size from one inch to as large as six feet, are endlessly tumbled by the river current, which makes them rounded and polished. Their striations and coloring are peculiar to the region. Even a pebble from these stones is believed to be an incarnation of the God Shiva and is regarded as symbolic of his supreme creative powers. The stones are often placed in special shrines dedicated to the Lord Shiva and are symbolic of his fertile powers. The Shiva Lingams are only accessible during the dry season and are only harvested from the river by select families

---

[283] Bourke, *op. cit.*, 18-19.
[284] Jones, David E. *Sanapia: Comanche Medicine Woman.* New York: Holt, Rinehart and Winston Case Studies in Cultural Anthropology, 1972, 96.

that are trained in recognizing them. The stones symbolize not only male fertility but also the feminine creative energy. In Hindu tradition, the lingam is regarded as the shape of the soul and is associated with the Fifth Chakra. The stones are not only regarded as energy generators, but also as healers.

An example of Shiva's Lingam Stone.

The Powers of Holed Stones

It is an ancient and almost universal custom to attribute special properties to stones that are naturally pierced with holes. The Radfords noted, "in almost every country of the world the same superstition prevailed, though there could have been no collusion of the peoples, and no knowledge the one of the other of the superstition. It is, again, the instance of some curious instinct and fear of men of all colours and races leading them to one general belief or trust in an unseen power." [285]

Passing through large, pierced stones is a ritual commonly seen throughout the world's folk medicine traditions. In Greece and Scotland, women desiring children would wade into the sea and then pass through large water-worn holes in nearby rocks. This practice is known from the Middle East to the Orient, with some similarities found in the United States and elsewhere. It is seen as an act of passing through dimensions, in an attempt to "pass on" or transfer illnesses and to obtain power and health. "Pregnant women of Kilghane in County Cork," wrote Aubrey Burl, "passed clothing through such a hole to ensure an easy childbirth."[286] Other traditions included men and women clasping hands through stone holes to swear their troth. It has been suggested that "the wedding ring...may represent the ultimate reduction of the original idea, where finally only a finger is passed through." [287]

There is evidence that prehistoric people would pass the bones of their dead through holed stones that had been erected in the entryways of chambered tombs. These tombs were regarded as portals to the otherworld. Carved standing stones were erected as recently as 750 years ago at Tiya, in Ethiopia, to mark burial sites. The buried section of the stones usually had holes in them to symbolize the passage of the soul from life to death.

Another ritual, focused on life instead of death, was acted out in modern times in Saintongue, France. Folklorist

---

[285] Radford, Edwin and Mona A. *Encyclopaedia of Superstitions.* New York: The Philosophical Library, 1949, 149.

[286] Burl, Aubrey. *Prehistoric Avebury.* New Haven: Yale University Press, 1979, 36.

[287] Hand, Wayland D. *Magical Medicine.* Berkeley: University of California Press, 1980, 148.

Wayman D. Hand noted that the women of this village "passed their newborn infants through holes in dolmens to guard them against evil, present and future." [288]

Putting parts of oneself through certain monuments was thought to prevent illness and evil and also to allow an individual to obtain forgiveness of sins. A stone scroll at Chela, Morocco, is placed about three feet from the ground so that visitors may easily insert their hands in a hole situated in its center. By doing so, they believe, they will have their sins forgiven.

In the Scottish fishing village of Applecross, a stone circle with a holed stone in the center was used as the community meeting place for both Christian worship and "ritual of a pagan nature." Worshippers would place their heads through the hole in the hopes of obtaining good omens. [289] The locals used the holed stone so often for prophetic purposes that the Presbytery in 1656 condemned the users.

Small stones with naturally-occurring holes in them have been especially prized for their purported magical properties and in many cases, they were believed to be linked directly to the Goddess. In North Carolina, at least through the 1920s, holed stones were worn by pregnant women to ease childbirth and in Northumberland up to the early 20th century holy, or holed, stones were placed around a horse's neck to protect it from disease. It was a common belief in the Ozarks that stones with naturally-occurring holes could ward off witches and evil spirits. It was also believed that such a stone tied to the bedpost would prevent nightmares.

On the Isle of Sheppey, in Britain, it was the custom to hang "such a stone, or even a beach stone, round the neck of

---

[288] Ibid.
[289] Lamont-Brown, Raymond. *Scottish Folklore*. Edinburgh: Birlinn Limited, 1996, 54.

every child until it reached its first birthday, but never afterwards," [290] for continued protection from disease.

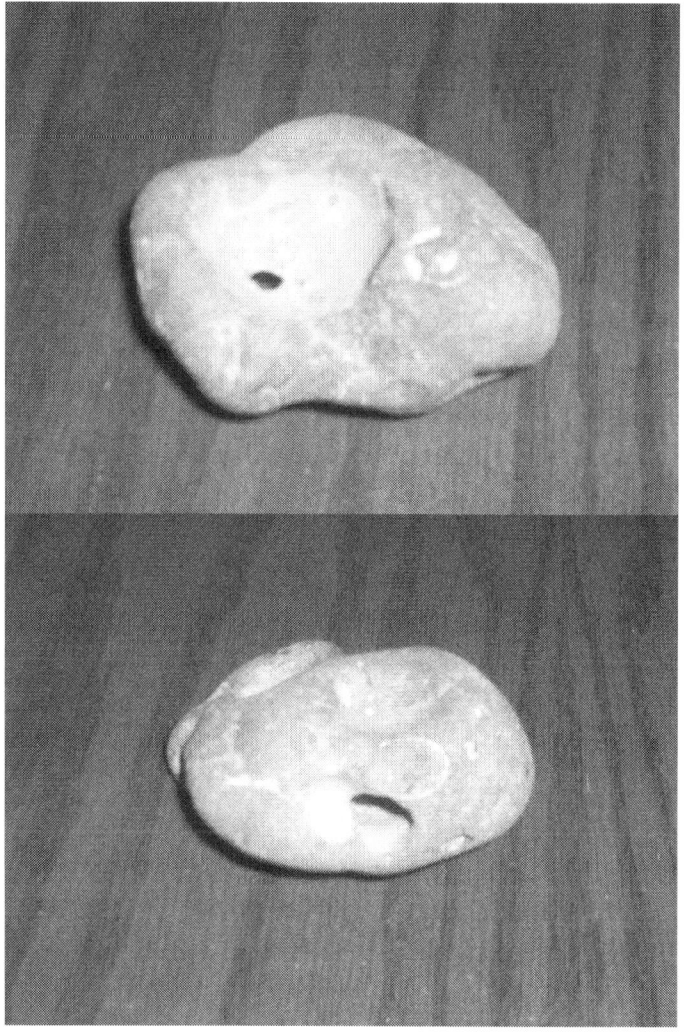

Two views of a naturally shaped and holed stone commonly used as an amulet (stone is 2 x 3").

---

[290] Radford *op. cit.* 228.

The Lakota Indian myth about Wohpe, who is an Earth Mother figure, and Okaga, the South Wind, speaks of Wohpe giving a magical holed stone to Okaga: "Here is a stone. Take and keep it. When you see it, think of me. It will keep you warm and if you wish a fire, rub it and fire will come from it. When you wish to forget me, throw it from you and you will remember me no more." [291] In another version of this story it is Waziyata, the North Wind, who gives Okaga a small black stone that will accomplish whatever task he wishes and will protect him when danger is near.

One of the most famous holed stone is that of Men-an-Tol, near the healing well of St. Madron's in Cornwall, England. At least through the 18th century and most probably well beyond that time, persons with back and limb pains would crawl through the hole in hopes of a cure. Children with rickets were also passed through the stone. For relief from pain, the individual had to pass through the hole either three or nine times, against the sun — or "widdershins." Children with rickets could only be cured if they were passed through to an adult of the opposite sex. Local folklore states that the Men-an-Tol had a protective Faery or Pixy in residence and it was this creature that would cure those who passed through the stone hole. In addition to cures, the benevolent Faery would also undo the work of evil Faeries and reverse a changeling into its human baby form. The November 28, 1868 issue of *Notes and Queries* reported that as late as 1749 offerings were being left at this holed stone. "Two pins," the article relates, were found on the top edge of the stone, "carefully lay'd across each other." Such pin offerings were commonly left at holy wells to appease the resident Faery, so we may assume similar beliefs were involved at Men-an-Tol.

---

[291] Walker, James R., ed by Elaine A. Jahner. *Lakota Myth*. Lincoln: University of Nebraska Press, 1983, 68.

Another important holed stone is the Tolvan Stone, also in Cornwall. At the Tolvan Stone, children were passed through the hole nine times, back and forth. To ensure that a cure had been obtained, it was imperative that, on the ninth pass, the child go round on the side where a grassy mound was located. The last part of the ritual was to lay the child to sleep on the mound with a sixpence under his or her head.

Smaller naturally-holed stones were hung in stables, cowsheds and homes to keep them safe "from witches, and were believed to protect horses and cattle from being ridden at night to the sabbats...."[292] This practice was used widely from Scotland through Cornwall to keep frogs and other pests from entering homes.

Holed stones and sacred wells are two features that have had the most universal and timeless following among humankind's ancient popular customs. Patterns of related beliefs can be found from India to Indiana, and the fact that they are so widespread indicates that a belief system existed which surely pre-dates the erection of the huge megaliths.

New mothers in Armenia who had difficulty breastfeeding frequented certain holy stones that were naturally shaped like breasts. According to Lalayan, the women would be taken to these sites, where they would drink the water that dripped from the stone and wash their own breasts with the water. Afterwards, they would pray and light candles in front of the stones. [293]

---

[292] Merrifield, Ralph. *The Archaeology of Ritual and Magic.* New York: New Amsterdam Books, 1987, 162.
[293] Opler, Morris Edward. *An Apache Life-Way: The Economic, Social, and Religious Institutions of the Chiricahua Indians.* Chicago: University of Chicago Press, 1941, 405.

Healing Stones

Stones were used to treat a variety of complaints and illnesses including mumps, insanity, rheumatism, consumption, and, of course, warts. Warts evidently have been a bane of humankind from the very beginning – and they were treated both at holy wells and at sacred rocks. For the most part, warts were treated via the transference method, by rubbing them with a pin and tossing the pin into a holy well, or rubbing them with rock and tossing the rock away. One ritual recorded in Ohio involved counting the number of warts and collecting the same number of small stones in a small bag. Then the instructions said to "go to the intersection of a road, throw the bag over your left shoulder, and return home by another way. The person who picks up the bag of stones will get your warts."[294] Other varieties of this tradition say that the warts are to be rubbed with the stones first and that the bag should be tied with a red bow.

Another cure, also from Ohio, says to rub warts with a stone and bury it at the first crossroads encountered. This method was commonly used in Great Britain and Western Europe as well. We see in these two examples that road intersections, or crossroads, are important for the cure to work. Why this should be held to be so important for the treatment of warts in particular is unknown, but the crossroads are indicative of a much more magical power. Symbolically, the crossroads represent the meeting place of time and space where magic takes place and where demons also meet. It is a dangerous place.

---

[294] Puckett, Newbell Niles. *Popular Beliefs and Superstitions: A Compendium of American Folklore from the Ohio Collection of Newbell Niles Puckett*, ed. by Wayland D. Hand. Boston: G K Hall & Co, 1981, 498.

A Scottish antidote called for the warts to be washed in water collected in natural basins found in "old 'layer' stones." These "layer stones" are assumed to be sedimentary rocks. After washing, the warts would disappear.

Mumps were given a special treatment. According to writer Lady Wilde, nine black stones had to be gathered before sunrise and the patient brought to a holy well with a rope around his neck. It was imperative that no one speak during the journey to the holy well. Once there, the patient was to "cast three stones in the name of God, three in the name of Christ, and three in the name of Mary. Repeat this process for three mornings and the disease will be cured." [295]

Bothered by insomnia? Among the "Pennsylvania Dutch," during the first two decades of the 20th century, it was said that sleep was sure to follow if the insomniac put a small round stone, found lying on a fencepost, under the pillow. [296] One wonders whether, as good neighbors, people were in the habit of placing round stones on fence posts just in case a needy person might pass by. A "sleeping stone" and a "waking stone" were also used in the 19th century. Reportedly, if a small number of sleeping stones were hung around a person's neck, the person would sleep straight through for three days and nights. The waking stone, on the other hand, would keep an individual awake without any ill effects and was said to be excellent for night watchmen.

Nine stones taken from a stream were used to bring down swelling of any kind, including stings. A different stone was taken each day for nine days and returned to the stream after its use. Similar treatments were common in both Chile and

---

[295] Wilde, Lady. *Irish Cures, Mystic Charms & Superstitions.* New York: Sterling Publishing Co., Inc., 1991, 24.
[296] Fogel, Edwin Miller. "Beliefs and Superstitions of the Pennsylvania Germans" in *Americana Germanica* (Philadelphia), 18 (1915), 268.

ancient Rome. The number nine is frequently associated with healing and divination lore around the world. Nine was connected with potent magic. Hopper noted that the number nine "invokes the favor of the triple triad of the angels and at the same time enlists the power of the devil." [297]

Likewise, the number three has held a special value in various rituals. Three is one of the most powerful numbers of religio-magic traditions. In the British Isles, it was common to use three stones in healing rituals. William Black noted in particular that wise-woman Margaret Sandieson took but "thrie small stones and twitched her head thrie tymes with everie one of them"[298] when she treated an ill woman. A similar method was also used in Scotland.

Storaker reported a cure for illness that involved having a woman healer heat three small stones, drop them into water and then have the patient drink the water. [299]

Bonwick noted that in Ireland, "down to a late period," people would pour water on the surface of stone "temples" and drink it, "that the draught might cure their diseases. Molly Grime, a rude stone figure, kept in Glentham church, was annually washed with water from Newell well…babies were sprinkled at cairns in Western or South Scotland down to the seventeenth century. Some stones were kissed by the faithful, like the Druid's Stone in front of Chartres Cathedral, once carefully kept in the crypt." [300]

---

[297] Hopper, Vincent Foster. *Medieval Number Symbolism: Its Sources, Meaning, and Influence on Thought and Expression.* Mineola: Dover Publications, Inc. 2000, 123.
[298] Black, William George. "Folk Medicine: A Chapter in the History of Culture". London: *Publications of the Folk-Lore Society #12, 1883*, 118.
[299] Storaker, Joh. Th. "Sygdom og Forgjo/relse I den Norske Folketro." *Norsk Folkeminnelag* No. 20. Oslo, 1932, 32.
[300] Bonwick, James. *Irish Druids and Old Irish Religions.* New York: Barnes and Noble Books 1894, 217.

Stonehenge may be the largest "healing stone" in the world. Geoffrey of Monmouth wrote in the 12th century that the megaliths had gained a reputation for the healing of many diseases. Again, the combination of water and stone becomes evident as Geoffrey notes that the stones were washed and the water used in baths for the ill. The healing attributed to Stonehenge was accepted well into the 17th and 18th centuries. Similarly, the "12 o'clock" stone, a large standing stone in Cornwall, was reputed to cure children of rickets — as long as they were not illegitimate or the offspring of "dissolute" parents.

Other healing stones from the past include the Red Stone in Perthshire, which was used to cure distemper; and the Lee Stone, owned by the Earl of Douglas, that kept plague away. The Lee stone was "rented out" for a hefty sum that was paid as a security deposit for its safe return. Other stones include the Murrain Stone, which was used into the 1890s and was dipped into water that was given to cattle in order to cure murrain (a term given for any infectious disease of cattle) and hydrophobia; and a charm stone from Ireland which was renowned for healing wounds — as long as it never touched English soil. This stone was taken by basket from patient to patient and rubbed on the wound to effect healing.

Thunderstones

Thunderstones are stones found throughout the Old World that are associated with lightning strikes. Thunderstones, in reality, were Stone Age[301] tools, such as

---

[301] These "thunderstones", or hand axes, were created at least 500,000 years ago and continued to be used in parts of Africa until approximately 50,000 years BCE. The "Stone Age" generally is defined as beginning approximately 2.5 million

hand axes. Some accounts state that they are always black in color with white streaks running through them — as, apparently, some axes were. They were deemed to have great power for healing and giving strength. They were used in the treatment of jaundice, lameness, cataracts, convulsions, consumption, goiter, and snakebite, in childbirth and, carried on the person, to relieve rheumatism. Neolithic stone axes must, indeed, have mystified people who came along later; they did not look like something that would have occurred in nature, and it would be impossible to explain how they came to litter the landscape. Inevitably, they were endowed with supernatural powers that even aristocratic churchmen would extol:

> He who carries one will not be struck by lightning, nor will houses if the stone is there; the passenger on a ship traveling by sea or river will not be sunk by storm or struck by lightning; it gives victory in law-suits and battles, and guarantees sweet sleep and pleasant dreams. —Marbodaeus, Bishop of Rennes, 12th century. [302]

The uses for these stone-axe "thunderbolts" in the Old World were numerous; they were tossed into wells to ensure a continuous supply of good water; they were placed in cattle troughs to protect cattle from disease; and water in which the stone had been boiled was used as a treatment for rheumatism.

These artifacts were probably seen as supernatural objects as long ago as the Iron Age, when memories of stone tools

---

years ago and lasting in some parts of the world yet today. See the appendix for a time-line that illustrates the prehistoric periods and associated megaliths.

[302] Merrifield, *op. cit.*, 11.

had already faded away. [303] In France, prehistoric stone axes were referred to as "witches fingers," lending them an obviously sinister quality. Small projectile points that were found during the Middle Ages were similarly viewed as supernatural in origin; people called them "elfshot," on the premise that they were arrow points made and fired by elves.

Folklore in Surinam says that, should one bathe in water containing a black thunderstone, enormous strength would be obtained. In fact, it is said that a man may become so strong that he can kill another with one blow — if the stone is dark enough. The darker the stone, the more potent it becomes. [304]

The Lore of Mystical Stones

Stones, in themselves steeped in myth and hidden meaning, are inextricably linked to sacred water. Ancient standing stones and sacred waters have a common ancestry. Their existence is intricately interwoven.

"Rain rocks" utilized by Native American shamans were intended to control the weather, especially rain and snow, and they were prized as well for their ritual ties to the Grizzly Bear. Standing stones erected by ancient Britons are perched high above important water sites in Ireland, such as the five-stone circle at Uragh, County Kerry, situated above the Cloonee Lough Upper and Lough Inchiquin. Large rock outcroppings decorated with carvings and painting rise high above similarly hallowed water sources in the American West.

Individuals still feel an inspiration to create rock monuments on or near water. A rather mysterious creation of

---

[303] *Ibid.*, 15.
[304] Penard, A.P. and T.E. Penard. "Popular Notions Pertaining to Primitive Stone Artifacts in Surinam," in *Journal of American Folklore*, 30 (1917), 260.

several dozen rock cairns was recently found along a sand bar on the American River in the middle of Sacramento, California. Obviously, these cairns are not an ancient construction — as the ebb and flow of the river in flood conditions would have destroyed them. Who created them, and why, is unknown but we can presume there was a certain primeval urge to create a special, physical link between the human and the spirit world, associated with the nature of water and stone.

Also in California, at Panther Meadows, mid-way up Mt. Shasta's 14,000-foot slope, rock cairns are in use even now by Native Americans who still regard the site as a spiritual center. Rock cairns have been used since time began, around the world, to mark migration trails of game, places of death or burial, landing sites for seamen, water sources and holy sites. The Cree say that when someone creates a small cairn out of a few rocks, "it grows, no one knows how, rock by rock." [305]

In Finland, the Stone of Pain was situated at the confluence of three rivers and the "spirit" of pain was believed to reside there. Pilgrims would visit the spot to request relief from their painful physical conditions. The combined power of the three rivers and the stone were construed as creating an ideal source for healing. "Stones of Pain" were actually cup stones that are widely found in Finland and around the world. These "cups" were shallow depressions carved into stone and were referred to as "Stones of Pain" as they were believed to absorb illness and pain. The Stone of Pain mentioned above was a specific cup marked stone located in a particularly important area.

---

[305] Kehoe, Alice B. and Thomas F. Kehoe. *Solstice-Aligned Boulder Configurations in Saskatchewan.* Canadian Ethnology Service Paper No. 48. Ottawa: National Museums of Canada, 1979, 37.

Water is associated with ancient stone circles, too, such as those found on or near Pobull Fhinn on Loch Langass in the Hebrides, Uneval, Kintraw, Argyll, Kockadoon, Co. Mayo, and Killadangan, Co. Mayo (all in the British Isles), among the hundreds situated around the world.

Sacred stones in association with specific holy wells are also common. One such well-stone combination is found at Whitstone, England. Whitstone is a name derived from a white rock located on the south side of the nearby Whitstone church. R.A. Courtney, a noted pre-World War I antiquarian, wrote, "The Church is dedicated to St. Nicholas, and in the churchyard is a well commonly known as St. Anne's well. It is said to never have been known to fail; and it would show that the Church is but the successor of the sacred white stone; the water from the well being used for baptisms. It may be remarked that the saint of the Church is a male, the well a female; and, if my theory is correct, the stone represented the lingam, the well the yoni."[306]

The Hupa Indians of Northern California ritually washed certain standing stones called "story people" in the belief that the act of washing them could change the weather.[307] Similarly, the fishermen on the Isle of Skye washed certain stones to improve weather conditions. W. Winwood Reade, in his classic book *The Veil of Isis, or Mysteries of the Druids*, wrote, "in a little island near Skye is a chapel dedicated to St. Columbus; on an altar is a round blue stone which is always moist. Fishermen, detained by contrary winds, bathe this stone in water, expecting thereby to obtain favorable winds; it

---

[306] Courtney, R.A. *Cornwall's Holy Wells: Their Pagan Origins*. Penzance: Oakmagic Publications, 1997, 30.

[307] These stones were situated in rows. Heizer wrote, "when frosts come in the fall…a man or a virgin takes a basket of water with incense root and washes all these stones, praying…that gentle rain may come and that the frost may go away" (see "Sacred Rain Rocks of Northern California").

is likewise applied to the sides of people troubled by stitches, and it is held so holy, that decisive oaths are sworn upon it." [308]

An account of a "Pagan idol" from the Irish island of Inniskea, off the coast of Mayo, wrapped in flannel, was given in the *Notes and Queries* issue of Saturday, February 7, 1852:

> A stone carefully wrapped up in flannel is brought out at certain periods to be adored; and when a storm arises, this god is supplicated to send a wreck on their coast.
>
> Though nominally Roman Catholics, these islanders have no priest resident among them; they know nothing of the tenets of that church, and their worship consists in occasional meetings at their chief's house, with visits to a holy well called Derivla. The absence of religion is supplied by the open practice of pagan idolatry. In the south island a stone idol called in the Irish Neevougi, has been from time immemorial religiously preserved and worshipped. This god resembles in appearance a thick roll of homespun flannel, which arises from the custom of dedicating to it a dress of that material whenever its aid is sought; this is sewed on by an old woman, its priestess. Of the early history of this idol no authentic information can be procured, but its power is believed to be immense; they pray to it in time of sickness, it is invoked when a storm is desired to dash some hapless ship upon their coast, and again it is solicited to calm

---

[308] Reade, W. Winwood. *The Veil of Isis, or Mysteries of the Druids.* North Hollywood: Newcastle Publishing Company, 1992, 228.

the waves to admit of the islanders fishing or visiting the main land. [309]

Can we make a connection with this flannel cloth made by a priestess to adorn a sacred stone and the strips of cloth that still adorn wells and trees that are held sacred? The association of the stone and the holy well is, again, indicative of many sites throughout the British Isles. The stone is also anciently associated with sacred wells and this account may record one of the truly authentic Pagan practices that survived in Ireland into the 19th century.

"Rain rocks" were utilized by shamans as tools to control rain and weather. Rain rocks in Northern California were inscribed with meandering lines, grooves, cupules and carvings of bear claws and paw prints.

The Shasta Indians in the Klamath River area carved long parallel grooves on rain rocks to make the snow fall, and cupolas to produce rain. To stop rain, they covered the rain rock with powdered incense-root. According to rock art researcher Campbell Grant, the Hupa Indians of California "had a sacred rain rock called *mi*. By this rock lived a spirit who could bring frost, prolong the rainy season, or cause drought if he was displeased." [310] The Hupa would cook food next to the rain rock and provide a feast for the spirit to ensure that the spirit would continue to help them.

Rain rocks were fairly universal among early cultures. In Australia's Northern Territory, it was "essential" for certain types of rocks to be scratched to ensure rain.[311] Although they are rarely found in Southern California, a five-foot rain rock

---

[309] Tennent, Sir J. Emerson. *Notes and Queries*, Vol. V, No. 119, Saturday, February 7, 1852, 121.
[310] Grant, op. cit., 31.
[311] Mulvaney, D.J. *The Prehistory of Australia*. New York: Frederick A. Praeger, Publishers, 1969, 172.

marked with hundreds of small, drilled holes has been discovered on the slopes of Palomar Mountain in northern San Diego County. The site was a proto-historic Luiseño village, known as Molpa. [312] Just below the rain rock is a small spring, which was a steady source of water. Because the decoration or alteration of rock material is difficult to date, we cannot determine when the use of "rain rocks" began. We do know that the Tolowa, Karok and Hupa tribes on the North Coast of California used rain rocks to control the weather at least from 1600 CE, and the practice continued into the early 1800s — and may in fact continue today. [313]

The use of special stones to create rain appears to be a fairly universal practice. Rain-stones were used by the Samoan Islanders, Australian aborigines, by people in Central Africa, Japan, and Great Britain, as well as in North America. In most cases these stones were dipped into or sprinkled with water by priests or shamans and were treated to elaborate rituals. Sir James Frazer wrote that in northwestern Australia,

> "the rain-maker repairs to a piece of ground which is set apart for the purpose of rain-making. There he builds a heap of stones or sand, places on the top of it his magic stone, and walks or dances round the pile chanting his incantations for hours, till sheer exhaustion obliges him to desist, when his place is taken by an assistant. Water is sprinkled on the stone and huge fires are kindled. No

---

[312] True, D.L., C.W. Meighan & Harvey Crew. *Archaeological Investigations at Molpa, San Diego County, California*. University of California Publications in Anthropology, Volume 11, Berkeley: University of California Press, 1974.

[313] Clewlow, Jr., C. William & Mary Ellen Wheeling. *Rock Art: An Introductory Recording Manual for California and the Great Basin*. Los Angeles: Institute of Archaeology, University of California, 1978, 21-22.

layman may approach the sacred spot while the mystic ceremony is being performed." [314]

In North America, the Apache Indians in Arizona would carry water from specific springs and throw it on the top of a certain rock. "After that," Frazer continues, "they imagine that the clouds would soon gather, and that rain would begin to fall." [315] Rain-stones were used in similar ways during times of draught in ancient Rome as well. The stone called lapis manalis was kept near the Temple of Mars and "dragged into Rome, and this was supposed to bring down rain immediately." [316]

Just what is the power in these stones that is believed to cause rain? In most instances, the stone was thought to contain the spirit of divinity or act as a conduit to the divine, who could be supplicated via the stone.

A Chinese tale recorded by Pu Songling, in the 17th century, tells of a "Rare Stone from Heaven." The stone, described as "one foot in diameter, exquisite from all angles with picturesque ridges and peaks," had the ability to forecast rain. According to the tale, "whenever it was about to rain, clouds would emerge from each of its holes, which looked from the distance like new cotton stuffed in its openings." Many sought to get their hands on this stone, and all experienced disaster when they tried to possess it. [317]

Stones were used in many parts of the world to control not only rain, but also wind. In New Guinea, a "wind stone" was struck with a stick; the strength of the wind would vary depending on how hard the stone was struck. "In Scotland,"

---

[314] Frazer, Sir James. *The Golden Bough: A Study in Magic and Religion.* Hertfordshire: Wordsworth Editions Ltd., 1993, 76.
[315] Ibid.
[316] *Ibid.*, 78.
[317] Songling, Pu. *Selected Tales of Liaozhai.* Beijing: Panda Books, 1981, 133.

says Frazer, "witches used to raise the wind by dipping a rag in water and beating it thrice on a stone, saying:

> I knok this rag upon this stone
> To raise the wind in the divellis name,
> It shall not lye till I please againe. [318]

Frazer also notes that at Victoria, British Columbia, "there are a number of large stones not far from what is called the Battery. Each of them represents a certain wind. When an Indian wants any particular wind he goes and moves the corresponding stone a little; were he to move it too much, the wind would blow very hard." [319]

Both in the United States and Britain individual stones in association with water traditionally are said to cure illnesses. If you suffer from cramps while swimming you should pick up a few stones, spit on them and throw them into the water. A Norwegian technique to cure an illness is to take a stone from a hill, one from a field and a third from a crossroad (without touching them with your bare hand, though), heat them and drop them into water. The individual then must sit over the water, with a blanket covering his head. [320] In Ireland, unusually shaped stones found near holy wells are believed to be imbued with healing power. When an individual was too ill to visit the well, one of these stones would be borrowed in hopes of obtaining a cure.

Stones also were seen as containing spirits and could be the homes of Rock Babies, Faeries and other citizens of the

---

[318] Frazer, Sir James. *The Magic Art and the Evolution of Kings, Vol. 1.* London: Macmillan & Co Ltd., 1955, 322.
[319] Ibid.
[320] Storaker, Joh. Th. "Sygdom og Forgjo/relse I den Norske Folketero" in *Norsk Folkeminnelag No. 20.* Oslo, 1932, 31.

Underworld. Relating folk beliefs in Norway, Storaker wrote, in 1928:

> It was once believed that one could see the soul of a person as a small flame burning with a clear light. Such a light is often seen from stones. But usually, such a light from the stones is believed to be lit by the spirits living in the stone, and it is burning during the night. When the spirits of the stones appear like that, they are given the names of goblins, gnomes or subterraneans. The light looks like the light that is often seen at mounds, and which is called mound-light or spirit-light. [321]

Apparently, even Storaker was not quite sure how rational he wanted to be in reporting on this "spirit-light" or "mound-light." He speaks about the lights without apparent question or irony, even while he treats the original premise of souls appearing as flames in stone as simple "old wives-tales." Storaker also noted that, "occasionally one would see a light burning in some stone, especially at the darkest time of the year. The light came from some creatures that had lived in the stones." If the location was examined carefully, Storaker wrote, sometimes a small, round stone would be found which could be used by a "wise woman" to cure an illness. [322]

Similar tales are also found in Wales. On Innis-na-Gore, in the early 20th century, there was a large rock around which a "mysterious light" would suddenly appear in the night. The property owner decided to blow the rock up in an attempt to determine the source of the light. What he found, according to the story, was a Druid "enchantment," that is, a Druid waiting

---

[321] Storaker, Joh. Th. "Naturrigerne I den Norske Folketro" in *Norsk Folkeminnelag No 18*. Oslo, 1928, 12.
[322] *Ibid.*, 14.

to be released from the stone. The story states that a local priest did away with the object before release could be obtained.

In his work, *Celtic Folklore,* John Rhys speaks of a stone that gave light. He repeats a bit of folklore about a shepherd boy who became lost in the mist on a mountain while tending his flock. He met an "old fat man" who was really a Faery. The two walked on until they came to an oval stone, which the old man lifted up and tapped three times with his walking-stick. Upon the last tap, the stone produced light that varied in brightness from white, to gray to blue. The Faery, with his glowing stone, led the boy on and on until they came to the Land of Enchantment where the boy stayed a year and a day among the Faery-folk.

Spirits who inhabited stone were a subject in folktales in Belgium, as well. Spence noted a "particularly fearsome ghost story...in which it is related how certain spirits had become enclosed in a pillar in an ancient abbey..." [323] And fearsome "eating ghosts" that would eat the soul of a passerby were believed to inhabit certain long stones in the Banks Islands in the Caribbean. Likewise, the Faery were said to inhabit, or "ensoul," the standing stones of Brittany. It is likely that the Faery were also assumed to be the spirits of dead ancestors awaiting their next incarnation. Icelandic folklore speaks of trapping ghosts under rocks, where they remain until someone removes the stone. (This is certainly one method to "ensoul" the stone.[324]) A ritual still conducted every year in Shebbear, Devon, is called "Turning the Devil's Boulder." To ensure that the village remains protected, the villagers meet

---

[323] Spence, Lewis. *Legends and Romances of Brittany.* Mineola: Dover Publications, Inc., 1997, 52.
[324] Simpson, Jacqueline. *Icelandic Folktales and Legends.* Berkeley: University of California Press, 1972, 135.

after nightfall each November 5th with crowbars to turn over a large boulder that reportedly had trapped the Devil. The ritual is believed to be an ancient one. It is obvious that the boulder did not originate in the area, as no similar type of stone exists there; it appears to have been transported over some distance for some ritualistic purpose—or the stone was naturally disloged from its original resting space and moved by glacial action.[325]

The concept that human spirits existed in stone is one that has had a wide following from the Mesolithic Azilian culture to a contemporary Mesolithic society — the Australian Arunta people. These two cultures believed that the spirits of the dead could be preserved in decorated stones.

In Europe, the Mesolithic (or middle Stone Age) era extended roughly from 10,000 to 4,000 years ago, ending with the introduction and widespread practice of agriculture. The Azilian culture was spread across northern Spain, England, France, Belgium, Holland, and Switzerland. A hunter-fisher society, the Azilian left little evidence of their religious traditions except the river cobbles that they engraved or painted with circles, points, lines, and human figures.

We do not know specifically what these cobbles meant to the Azilian; to some scholars, the markings on them suggest they represent an early form of markers, or possibly a notation of lunar cycles; but the similarities to the Aruntas' stones are too striking to ignore. Every Arunta tribe has a storehouse that protects their "churingas," painted pebbles, referred to as their "far distant ones." [326] The "far distant

---

[325] Glacial action is probably responsible for many of the odd stones found around the world that appear out of geologic context, however that does not mean that these stones were not later altered or used in ritual or religious observances or in the practice of folkmedicine.
[326] Spence, Lewis. *The Magic Arts in Celtic Britain.* Mineola: Dover Publications, Inc., 1999, 88.

ones" are the male and female spirits of their ancestors, carefully arranged in the cave storehouses of the tribe. "The churinga," according to Maringer, "is regarded as the embodiment of the dead person whose spirit and qualities are transferred to the present possessor."[327] In a cave in Switzerland, 133 Azilian stones were found broken. If these were "ancestor stones," researchers conjecture they were intentionally broken by an enemy group who, in effect, destroyed the souls of a tribe's ancestor population — an act of spiritual genocide. If they were a kind of cultural or economic archive, this act of vandalism may have represented the destruction of a people's most sophisticated attainment.

A secret society existing on New Britain, New Guinea would award each newly-initiated member a stone in the shape of a human or animal. The stone was believed to absorb the soul of the member and if the stone was broken, the individual was certain to die. [328]

The souls of the departed were also believed to enter stones in Hawaii. MacGregor noted the following in his 1932 ethnographic field notes:

> "When a person died and his spirit entered a stone, he was a tupu'a. People went to them and laid their troubles before them and they were assisted." [329]

Since its founding, the Christian Church has condemned "stone worship" — not simply because stones were stones, but because the particular stones represented other gods and

---

[327] Maringer, Johannes. *The Gods of Prehistoric Man*. London: The Phoenix Press 2002, 128.
[328] Frazer, *op. cit.* 680.
[329] http://www.hawaii.edu/oceanic/rotuma/os/MacGregor/McReligionStones.

supernatural powers, competitors to the God who had decreed "Thou shalt have no other gods before me."

As MacKenzie wrote, "the original Zeus was evidently worshipped as a stone pillar — the pillar which enclosed his spirit, or the spirit of his earthly representative, the priest king." [330] Likewise, the Earth Goddess was represented by a standing stone which was visited at certain times of the year, during certain phases of the moon, by women "who prayed for offspring."

Standing stones and stone circles, however, have a long tradition of being associated not only with gods but also with the Faery and the devil. Lewis Spence wrote in his 1945 publication, *The Magic Arts in Celtic Britain*, "standing stones in Brittany and other parts of that country are associated with fairies, who are thought of as inhabiting or 'ensouling' them." [331] Spence notes that the Faery probably represented "the spirits of dead chieftains once worshipped ancestrally." [332] In some cultures, the Faery are spirits waiting to be reborn. In Scotland it was said that the devil would appear in the center of any stone circle if one walks around the circle three times "against the sun" at midnight.

The Tolcarne Troll, a little old man dressed in a tight leather jerkin and hood, is reported to live inside the rock in an outcropping of greenstone on a hill above a church in Newlyn, Cornwall. Local tradition places his origin to the Phoenicians. Other names for him include "The Wandering One" and "Odin the Wanderer." [333]

---

[330] MacKenzie, Donald A. *Crete & Pre-Hellenic Myths and Legends*. London: Senate, 1995, 184.
[331] Maringer *op. cit.*
[332] Spence, *The Magic Arts in Celtic Britain*, 1999, 88.
[333] Evans-Wentz, W. Y. *The Fairy-Faith in Celtic Countries*. Mineola: Dover Publications, Inc. 2002, 176.

Native American lore is also rich in tales of divine stones. Walker recorded the following account from an old Lakota shaman:

"Tunkan is the spirit which fell from the sky. It is a stone. It knows all things which are secret. It can tell where things are when they are lost or stolen..." When children vanished, "the mysterious stones were consulted to learn what had become of the child."[334]

The Lakota utilized special shamans, called Rock Dreamers, to communicate with the Tunkan spirit. In the best case, the stone would tell the shaman where lost objects were, or, if they had been stolen, the identity of the individual who stole them. Some shamans use clear, round stones that are normally found on anthills to locate the bodies of the dead or to determine if an individual is still alive. The shaman asks the spirit of the stone to locate the person so that the family will be able to find them, or come to terms with the death. Rock dreamers were believed to take on some of the characteristics of stone, as well, such as being impervious to bullets. Because of this protection, the Rock dreamers were responsible for "war medicine."

Perhaps the most unusual magical stone is the Blaxhall Stone situated on the Stone Farm in Suffolk, England. The Blaxhall Stone grows. Reportedly, a hundred years ago, it was the size of a small loaf of bread, and today it weighs in at five tons. It is said to still be growing. Growing stones are also part of Hawaiian lore. According to folklorist Martha Beckwith porous pebbles found on the beach of Koloa on the island of Hawaii "were supposed to grow from a tiny pebble

---

[334] Walker, 1991, *op. cit.*, 112.

to a good-sized rock and to reproduce themselves if watered once a week."[335]

While stone worship is clearly out for Christians, stone lore has been used in Christian theology as examples of recommended Christian behavior. The 13th century Aberdeen Bestiary, written and illustrated in England around 1200 CE, speaks of "terrobolem" and how these stones indicate that man and woman should remain aloof from one another:

> "On a certain mountain in the east, there are fire-bearing stones which are called in Greek terrobolem; they are male and female. When they are far from each other, the fire within them does not ignite. But when by chance the female draws near to the male, the fire is at once kindled, with the result that everything around the mountain burns.
>
> "For this reason, men of God, you who follow this way of life, stay well clear of women, lest when you and they approach each other, the twin flame be kindled in you both and consume the good that Christ has bestowed upon you. For there are angels of Satan, always on the offensive against the righteous; not only holy men but chaste women too."[336]

Saints and Stones

Certain sacred and healing stones have become assimilated into Church lore and associated with particular saints. One example is St. Fillan, who was a 7th century

---

[335] Beckwith, Martha. *Hawaiian Mythology*. Honolulu: University of Hawaii Press 1970, 88
[336] McLaren, Colin, translator. *The Aberdeen Beastiary*. Aberdeen: Aberdeen University Library MS 24, 1995.

follower of St. Columba (known primarily for his holy well in Scotland). Into the 18th century, invalids would throw white stones on the saint's cairn as part of a ritual performed in their search of healing. This particular well also was said to move on its own and to cure insanity and other illnesses. The well is still frequented today. Those seeking a cure walk around the well three times and then throw a pebble into the well.

St. Fillan was the son of a princess of Ulster, who later became St. Kentigerna. His father was Prince Federach. Fillan was born with a stone in his mouth, a freak event which enraged (or horrified) his father. Prince Federach grabbed the infant and tossed him into a nearby lake (again the association between saints, water and sacred stones). A local Christian bishop just happened to be nearby (aren't they always, in these tales?) and rescued the baby. Out of gratitude, Fillan's mother became a Christian. [337] In time, Fillan and his mother became missionaries and traveled to Scotland where he established a priory in Auchtertyre at what is now Kirkton's Farm. One of the miracles for which St. Fillan became known was his ability to have his left arm and hand light up in the dark so he could read at night. Because of this, his arm has been preserved as one of the relics of that age in Glen Dochart, Scotland. (We do not know if it continues to serve as a flashlight or not.)

The most famous relics of St. Fillan are eight healing stones left to the monks at his priory. Like many talismans around the world, the stones are representative of body parts and are used by pilgrims to effect healing of the head (and sight, hearing, headaches, etc.), stomach, back and limbs. These eight stones are kept in an old mill at the priory site where, each Christmas Eve, they are given a new bed of straw and reeds from the river. Pilgrims are allowed to pick up the

---

[337] http://www.simegen.com/writers/nessie/stones.htm.

stones and rub them on afflicted body parts in hopes that St. Fillan's healing powers will work for them as well.

VIII
Amulets for Health

Amulets, charms and talismans have been used to take away illness and provide protection of the mind and body since antiquity. As described elsewhere in this book, amulets in the form of stones have a universal application and a universal appeal and have been used to treat illnesses as well as to avoid them.

Called *lithotherapy*, the use of stones in the treatment of diseases has included minerals, precious and semi-precious gems, coral and pearls, and stone-like objects said to have been produced in the bodies of both real and mythical creatures.

The *madstone* reportedly was recommended as a cure for both snakebite and rabies. There is still debate concerning what the madstone actually was. One example was said to have been found in the head of the cobre de capello and, when applied to a snake bite or poison arrow wound, would draw out the venom and then drop off the wound. Other forms of madstone include the famous Lee stone. According to legend, Sir Simon Lockhart of Lee fought the Saracens in the late 12th century and acquired a pebble set into a stone. "According to the story," writes Thomas Forbes, "water into which this talisman had been dipped would relieve fever, stop bleeding, and work other cures." [338] The Lee penny is known to have existed into the 19th century and was still used to treat dog bites. It had gained such a reputation for its

---

[338] Forbes, Thomas R. "The Madstone" in *American Folk Medicine: A Symposium*. Edited by Wayland D. Hand. Los Angeles: University of California Press 1976, 16.

healing powers that during the reign of Charles I it was borrowed by the city of Newcastle to combat the plague. The townspeople had to put up a bond of £6,000 to ensure its return.

Another healing amulet with a wide reputation is a large brown seed called the "petrified deer's eye" or *ojo de venado*. The seed is similar to a buckeye and in carried in Mexico to ward off evil spirits, which cause "bad air", or *mal aire*. Such "bad air" causes paralytic twitching and is brought on due to sudden exposure to rapid temperature changes or over heatedness caused by fits of anger. This condition has been linked to the Aztecs who believed that illness was caused by evil spirits present in the air.

An old tradition from California dating to the 1890s states that one should always carry a buckeye to ensure continued good health. This tradition continued well into the 1960s. A similar folk-medicine tradition existed in the Ozarks in the 1930s.

The wearing of amber was widely believed to prevent convulsions in children in 1950s Spain and folklore collected from Utah in the late 1960s indicate that amber beads worn around the neck also protected one against colds. Other illnesses said to be avoided with amber amulets include croup, goiter, whooping cough, pulmonary ailments, sore throat, asthma, enlarged thyroid, heart disease, nosebleed, and toothache among others. A word of caution, however, as amber amulets were also recommended to stop sexual desire.

Paine noted that amber, when rubbed, produces a slight electrical charge and a distinctive aroma which most likely contributed to the healing powers it was believed to hold. [339] "No doubt the early peoples, who gathered Adriatic and

---

[339] Paine, Sheila. *Amulets: Sacred Charms of Power and Protection.* Rochester: Inner Traditions 2004, 89.

Baltic amber and distributed it and its lore far and wide," wrote Donald Mackenzie, "discovered this peculiar quality in the sacred substance." [340]

Amber, like coral, shells and pearls, was thought to have originated in the seas and were closely associated with a goddess who, like Aphrodite, had her origins in the deep waters.

Jade is another amuletic stone widely used for its healing and protective properties. Jade has been used in India to cure reptile bite, although it is unknown how many of those bites were actually from venomous snakes. Jadeite was commonly used in folk-medicine in 16th century England for treating poisons. Anecdotal information indicates that by wearing jade, one can avoid kidney problems for a whole year. The Chinese would wear wristlets of jade to strengthen the arm and jade is reportedly a bringer of good luck and longevity.

In Mongolia, village shamans wore small amulets in the form of miniature blacksmith tools in their healing rituals. Coral is another substance used in protective amulets. Children wore pieces of "male and female" coral around their necks to be protected from the evil-eye in the 1940s. In Italy, coral pendants and red vests are still used to protect babies from the evil eye. In the 1880s coral was thought to "preserve and fasten the teeth of men" and was widely used to ease the pain of teething in children.

Coral traditionally has been regarded as the sea-tree of the Mother Goddess and the giver of life and fertility in waters. Coral was regarded as being the "life substance" of the goddess in ancient Egypt. In Greek myth, coral is grown from

---

[340] Mackenzie, Donald A. *Ancient Man in Britain.* London: Senate 1996, 164.

the blood of Medusa. [341] In Spain, amulets of coral were believed to protect children from convulsions.

Copper is an ancient amuletic material that is still commonly used today to ease arthritic pain and to provide a number of health benefits. Copper bracelets are sold through television advertisements as cure-alls for pains and illnesses and sell for as much as $150 each. They can also be bought in New Age shops and drug stores around the United States for as little as $1.50. Scientific tests on copper wire and bands of copper have shown no effectiveness in healing but amulets require faith more than scientific evidence to produce results. While copper was, and still is, most often recommended for arthritis and rheumatism, it has also been worn as a protective device against snake bite. Other uses include children wearing a copper penny around the neck until the child is old enough to talk to avoid speech defects. In addition, bee stings were said to be neutralized by placing a copper coin on the area stung. Those penny-loafers most likely carry old superstitions with them as well.

An old practice from the first few years of the 20th century included taking the copper pennies off the eye-lids of the deceased and using them as amulets against rheumatism.

The Egyptians undoubtedly used copper for magical purposes before they began to use it for jewelry and weapons. Many sacred wells and waterways received copper offerings and many of these wells still carry names such as "Penny well" and "pin well" which reflect these offerings.

Other, more mundane items that we use everyday have also been used as charms and amulets to prevent and cure illnesses and body pains. Folklorist W. J. Witemberg recorded in 1918 that an informant in Canada "gave to the author, to

---

[341] Cooper, J.C. *An Illustrated Encyclopaedia of Traditional Symbols.* London: Thames and Hudson Ltd. 1978, 42.

add to his collection of charms and amulets, a dried and hardened potato which he had carried on him for a year as a cure for rheumatism. A fresh potato, he explained, had to be put in one's pocket at the end of every year." [342]

Likewise, strings of garlic and onions were worn to remain healthy and should one carry an old lemon with them, it would also ensure good health.

Italian-Americans in the 1950s continued an ancient tradition to combat the evil eye. They wore small metal male hunchback figurines to combat this dreaded sorcery. It was believed that sickly female hunchbacks could cause the disease and the male hunchback figurines were able to combat it successfully.

In Germany during the 1950s crayfish eyes were credited with supernatural power and they were frequently made into amulets in the shape of the cross with 3 to 5 dried eyes or "stones." This concretion is not unlike that of the bezoar stone and is taken from the stomach of river crayfish. These crosses were frequently hung around the necks of children to ensure good health. It is unknown if this tradition continues today.

There are as many amulets, charms and talismans as there are ailments, despair and desires in the world. Leo Kanner wrote, "In short, heaven and earth and all three kingdoms of nature and God and a world of spirits and ghosts are involved in the subject of medical folklore." [343]

---

[342] Wintemberg, W. J. "Folk-Lore Collected in the Counties of Oxford and Waterloo, Ontario." Journal of American Folklore, 31 (1918), 135-153.
[343] Kanner, Leo. "Medical Folklore." Medical Life, 38, pt. 2 (1931), 523-527.

IX
Contemporary Use of Amulets & Charms

Crosses, the Star of David, the Egyptian ankh, the St. Christopher medal and the Wiccan pentacle are commonly worn amulets in contemporary society. Other more natural items also continue to be used to ward off evil, ensure health and fertility and bring luck.

Charms and amulets continue to be popular items even in the 21st century. They are used in much the same way and for the same reasons as they were in prehistoric times. Horseshoes are one of the most common forms and are often found on gates and fences and nailed to barn doors in the American west where horse ownership is widespread.

The origin of this tradition is an interesting one. Horseshoes, traditionally made from iron, thus effective against the Farey and Elves, are symbolic of courage, strength and power. Ralph Merrifield wrote in his study, *The Archaeology of Ritual and Magic*, "Horseshoes were not the only domestic charms then considered to be not merely 'lucky' but quite specifically antidotes to witchcraft."[344] Nailing a horseshoe to the barn door was believed to prohibit a witch from taking and riding a horse or cow to the midnight sabbats. This custom is found around the world in most agricultural societies or settings.

The horseshoe was also nailed to the masts of fishing vessels to protect them from storms. The horseshoe, however, must be hung with the ends pointing up in order to hold luck

---

[344] Merrifield, Ralph. *The Archaeology of Ritual and Magic.* New York: New Amsterdam Books 1987, 161.

in or, as the Radford's noted, to confuse the devil in his normally circular travels so that he must then "take a retrograde course." [345]

"'That the horseshoe may never be pulled from your threshold!' was one of the good wishes or 'sentiments' of the last century," wrote Frederick Elworthy in 1895, "and throws some light upon the unwillingness of my neighbour...to permit any disturbance of the protectors behind his door." [346]

In Tibet, charms made from twisted wool and paper serve the same purpose as horseshoes in the United States and Europe—to keep demons and witches away from horses and pony's. The charms are tied over each horse stall to provide needed protection.

The rabbit's foot is another "lucky amulet" that was common during the 1950s. The origin of the lucky rabbit's foot may lie in the "belief that young rabbits are born with their eyes open, and thus have the power of the Evil Eye, and can shoo away the Evil One." [347]

Writing in the 1940s, folklorists Edwin and Mona Radford stated, "a rabbit's foot is the most potent charm of the American negroes, who, it is said, turn white with fright at the loss of one." [348] However, they then go on to relate that the use was, at least in the 1940s, common in Britain and used by "hundreds of mothers" who placed one in their children's "perambulator" when taken out for a stroll to protect against any possible accident. Thousands of rabbit feet were made in the United States and exported to England carrying an advertisement stating that the foot was "the left hind foot of a

---

[345] Radford, Edwin and Mona A. *Encyclopaedia of Superstitions.* New York: Philosophical Library 1949, 151.
[346] Elworthy, Frederick Thomas. *The Evil Eye: The Classic Account of an Ancient Superstition.* Mineola: Dover Publications, Inc. 2004, 218.
[347] Radford, op cit, 195.
[348] Ibid.

rabbit killed in a country churchyard at midnight, during the dark of the moon, on Friday the 13th of the month, by a cross-eyed, left-handed, red-headed bow-legged Negro riding a white horse". This last statement had a convenient disclaimer — "this we do not guarantee." [349]

Thompson notes "Pepys mentions in his *Diary*, that he wore a hare's foot to avert the plague, and seems to have placed more faith in the amulet than in all the vaunted remedies that were recommended for that terrible scourge." [350]

A ritualized use of amulets occurs throughout the Old World, from the United Kingdom through Eastern Europe and the Mediterranean. The belief that trees are somehow supernatural beings is universal. Ozark lore says that agents of the Devil propagated the ironwood tree and that the sassafras tree does not grow from seeds, but rather they "somehow sprout from grub worms." [351] The belief in "Devil Trees" was common in Africa and the Malay Archipelago. However, these trees are receptacles of evil rather than sources of evil. Like the holy wells in England and elsewhere where people tie strips of cloth and ribbon, known as "clooties", to nearby trees, these Devil Trees are also sought out for this purpose. In both cases, the purpose is the same, to tie a piece of cloth that belongs to an ill person to the tree so that the disease is transferred from the human to the tree. The view that clooties may transfer ones disease to the host tree is common throughout the world, however another view is that

---

[349] *Folk-Lore* 19 (1908), 296.
[350] Thompson, C.J. S. *The Hand of Destiny: Folklore and Superstitions for Everyday Life.* New York: Bell Publishing Company 1989, 182. A reprint of the 1932 edition published by Rider & Company, London.
[351] Randolph, Vance. *Ozark Magic and Folklore.* New York: Dover Publications 1964, 261 (A reprint of *Ozark Superstitions* published by Columbia University Press 1947)

those who have been healed have left these tokens to the well's spirits in gratitude. This practice is still very much alive today and this author saw such offerings at St. Madron, Sancreed and St. Nectan's Falls in Cornwall in September 2000.

Clootie wells are common in Scotland, Ireland and particularly in Cornwall. However, wells called "Rag Well" are found in Dublin Ireland, Newcastle and Benton, both in Northumberland showing a wide distribution in Great Britain outside of Cornwall. In fact, this particular form of offering appears to be widespread throughout the world from Britain to Turkey to Mongolia. While some Clootie Wells are believed to function only as "wishing wells," most Clootie's are in reality healing wells. A common practice at the Clootie Wells in Scotland is that an individual wishing a cure must approach the well from the southeast, and drink three handfuls of water while wishing for the desired cure. At this time, a piece of cloth is attached to the tree. Should anyone remove the cloth, the troubles and illnesses of the pilgrim would be transferred to the person removing the cloth. When I visited several clootie wells in Cornwall there was no evidence that offerings had been removed, obviously the cautionary tales were well taken. Native American people, such as the Kitanemuk living in the Tehachapi Mountains, were also prone to leave offerings at sacred sites. They too believed that death would be the result for anyone stealing from the shrines.[352]

---

[352] Blackburn, Thomas C. and Lowell John Bean. "Kitanemuk", in *Handbook of the Indians of California: Volume 8-California.* Washington: Smithsonian Institution 1978, 568

Clootie tree, Cornwall, England.

Many of the cloth strips that I saw as votive offerings at holy wells in Cornwall were red or weathered pink in color. Logan wrote that red cloth was left for a wide variety of magical purposes:

"It is the color which is believed to resist the power of evil spirits…" [353]

Sheila Paine described one site in Central Asia with clootie trees: "Where the Mongols razed the ancient oasis cities of Central Asia, holy sites are marked by a tree bedecked with rags, such as the Forty Mullahs' Hill of Kunya Urgench in Tuekmenistan, littered with bones and skulls believed to be the remains of its massacred inhabitants. A spindly tree below the hill is almost obliterated by rags, and surrounded by

---

[353] Logan, Patrick. *The Holy Wells of Ireland*. Buckinghamshire: Colin Smythe 1980, 116

women hanging up more, as prayers for conception, white in hope of a boy, coloured for a girl." [354]

Crucifixes are commonly seen adorning women around the world—as well as men from certain ethnic backgrounds. But the cross has been used as a sacred symbol for thousands of years. They have been used for decorating the beaded saddle blankets of Native Americans as well as important symbols from ancient Babylon, throughout Africa and Asia and into Celtic and Hindu cultures.

Cooper noted that the cross "is the cosmic symbol par excellence" representing the world center and a point of communication between the heavens and the earth. [355]

The cross is a common motif in Native American art and symbolism, much as it is in many other cultures. Generally speaking, the arms of the cross represent the four cardinal directions. They represent the cosmic axis between heaven and earth; they also represent the dualism of nature.

In the Mayan world, the tau, or "T" cross is the Tree of Life and the Tree of Nourishment. The cross also represents the four winds and fertility. The cross is one of Quetzalcoatl's symbols as well.

In many Native American traditions, the earth has gone through several rebirths, with the earth and all of the creatures and plants on it evolving in periodic spurts of creation. To Mesoamericans, there are five suns, or eras of the world, four of these have already passed.

---

[354] Paine, Sheila. *Amulets: Sacred Charms of Power and Protection.* Rochester: Inner Traditions 2004, 142.
[355] Cooper, J.C. *An Illustrated Encyclopaedia of Traditional Symbols.* London: Thames and Hudson Ltd. 1978, 45.

Crow Woman's horse blanket, Sioux ca. 1890. Photograph courtesy Carnegie Museum of Natural History, Pittsburgh, Pennsylvania.

The four suns previously destroyed were the Sun of Night, which represented a sterile world of darkness and hopelessness; the Sun of Air, represented by Quetzalcoatl and indicative of pure spirit; the Sun of Rain and the Sun of Fire were the third and fourth eras. The Suns of Night and Air are the two higher eras and the Suns of Fire and Rain represent the two lower eras. The last Sun, the Sun of Movement is also known as the Sun of Quetzalcoatl and represents a time when man and spirit merge.

Mesoamericans, like other indigenous cultures, believe in a concept of unity and harmony between man and nature. The Aztecs believed that when the human era, known as the "Sun of Movement" ends, the spiritual growth of man will have been completed and humankind will join God.

The cross has been utilized in Mesoamerican symbolism to represent both Quetzalcoatl and Tlaloc. To the Nahuatl the cross represented solar power with the four points in the center of the cross symbolizing the meeting of man and the heavenly spirit. The center also symbolized the meeting place of "opposed principles."

The Nahuatl believed that in the center of existence the "supreme reality" resided. This "Law of the Center" was the basis of Toltec symbolism, which focused on Quetzalcoatl and his cross.

The cross also figured in preventive folk-medicine. The Ojibwa in Canada tattooed the cross on each cheek to prevent toothache and believed in a cause and effect relationship between the cross and good health.

When the Native American messianic Ghost Dance religion began in the late 1800s, the cross was often embroidered on "Ghost shirts" which were worn both in ritual and in battle. The Ghost shirts were believed to make the wearer impervious to bullets or other harm as well as to provide invisibility. Other symbols were also painted on the Ghost shirt or on the person in the form of circles and crescents. According to James Mooney a 19th century ethnologist, these symbols represented the sun, the moon and the morning star.[356]

The relationship between the cross and the "holy" or "magical" is quite obvious and universal. Paine wrote:

> "...when established religions begrudgingly took cognizance of pagan amulets," noted Paine, "Islam annexed the hand as a symbol, Christianity took the cross.

---

[356] Mooney, James. *The Ghost Dance Religion.* Chicago: University of Chicago Press 1965, 68.

Yacatecuhlti, the bearded patron god of travelers and merchants with his walking staff "cross," depicting the four directions.

"The positioning and application of the cross is diverse. Often it carries associations with the Church, though that the cross can be considered an amulet in the Christian context is debatable: God protects, not a symbol. However, a beleaguered Christian household in a society of Muslims or animists certainly believes that the cross they have placed on their roof, or painted over their door, acts as an amulet. Likewise, a crucifix made by the local blacksmith—well known to possess magic powers—will be hung on their wall to protect them." [357]

Other Christian amulets include the many saint's medals of the Catholic church such as the St. Christopher's medal. While the St. Christopher medal is worn to protect people on their travels, others, such as St. Anthony of Padua and St. Roch, were worn to protect cattle from witchcraft and people

---

[357] Paine, op cit., 167.

from the plague. In Belgium during the early years of the 20th century, religious medals were worn in the belief that they aided in the regulation of menstrual cycles.

The amulet shown below, a silver piece carried by followers of Maria Lionza, an indigenous goddess of Venezuela, offers the wearer love and good fortune. Religious medals, whether Christian or pagan, serve the same purpose. The cult of Maria Lionza dates back to the 16th century but is heavily influenced by Catholicism and followers of Santeria.

Religious amulet used by followers of Maria Lionza, Venezuela.

We can't, of course, forget the lucky penny! Most all of us have tossed a penny or coin into a fountain or pool "for luck" or to make a wish. The tradition of tossing coins into fountains and wells is an ancient one and still continues today. It is doubtful that many of us realize just how ancient our practice of tossing coins into "wishing wells" and ponds is. To some the act of tossing coins into holy water increases the power of the water to combat evil and to grant wishes.

Pliny the Younger wrote of the many coins glittering in the shallow waters of one of the Italian rivers. The obvious intent is to give up a possession of some value in exchange for something desired—be it health, wealth, love or some other item of value. Originally, it was an act of sacrifice. The coins we toss in a fountain today may not have the same value they did in far earlier times but the act is the same—even if the act of tossing the coins has become automatic rather than thought out.

In many areas of the world, coins are worn like jewelry and for the same reasons—as amulets protective against the evil eye. "Coins are a major feature of much traditional costume of the Balkans, Russia and Eastern Europe," writes Paine, "covering headdresses and bib fronts." [358]

Coins continue to be impaled on tree trunks as offerings to the tree spirits and gods and are often removed by other pilgrims and used as amulets. In the 1930s, Pennsylvania Germans would lay silver coins on wounds to prevent discoloration and contemporary folklore of the 1970s in the American southwest suggested that when a knife is given as a gift one should also give coins to prevent the person from being accidentally cut with the knife.

And, of course, dreaming of coins is a sign of good health and tradition dictates that if a coin is placed under the pillow of a small child it will grow to be successful.

---

[358] Paine, op cit., 96.

In some cultures, coins continue to be placed on the eyelids of the dead to prevent the spirit from reentering the body after death.

Coins may also buy a new bride years without children in Eastern Europe. The more coins she places in front of a picture of the Virgin Mary the more years she will have of married happiness without children.

Afterword

As shown in this book, people in every age and culture have sought out both everyday items and those rare and unusual creations of nature to obtain peace of mind, protection and good health—not to mention financial success.

Many times the items used are difficult to identify but most of the time they reflect natural but unusual items such as buckeyes, certain types of minerals and stones. Other times they are exquisitely made representations of gods and goddesses and religious concepts.

The extreme age of these sacred objects speak of the dawn of abstract thought, of the earliest attempt of humans to communicate and influence the gods and goddesses to ensure that the individual, the clan, the tribe was able to survive successfully against terrible odds.

The amazing thing about this story is that so many amulets and charms continue to be used in the same way and for the same purposes that they did in prehistoric times. It is man's attempt to find solace in a world not in his control, even though he likes to think it is. But really, does it hurt to carry a buckeye or an unusually shaped stone or a "lucky penny" in the quest for safety, good health and happiness? For hundreds of thousands of years most people have said that it is simply insurance; after all we need all the help we can get!

Bibliography

Andersen, Johannes C. *Myths and Legends of the Polynesians.* Rutland: Charles E. Tuttle Company, 1969

Baroja, Julio Caro. *The World of the Witches.* London: Phoenix Press 2001

Blécourt, William de. "The Witch, her Victim, the Unwitcher and the Researcher: The Continued Existence of Traditional Witchcraft" in *Witchcraft and Magic in Europe: The Twentieth Century.* Philadelphia: University of Pennsylvania Press 1999

Bourke, John G. *Apache Medicine-Men.* New York: Dover Publications, Inc. 1993

Briggs, Robin. *Witches & Neighbors: The Social and Cultural Context of European Witchcraft.* New York: Viking 1996

Budge, Sir E.A. Wallis. *Egyptian Magic.* New York: Dover Publications Inc. 1971

Burl, Aubrey. *Prehistoric Avebury.* New Haven: Yale University Press, 1979

Clewlow, Jr., C. William & Mary Ellen Wheeling. *Rock Art: An Introductory Recording Manual for California and the Great Basin.* Los Angeles: Institute of Archaeology, University of California, 1978

Cooper, J.C. *An Illustrated Encyclopaedia of Traditional Symbols.* London: Thames and Hudson Ltd. 1978

Cooper, John M. *Analytical and Critical Bibliography of the Tribes of Tierra del Fuego and Adjacent Territory.* Bureau of American Ethnology Bulletin 63. Washington: Smithsonian Institution 1917

Courtney, R.A. *Cornwall's Holy Wells: Their Pagan Origins.* Penzance: Oakmagic Publications, 1997

Cowan, R.A., Clewlow, C.W. Jr & et al. "An Unusual Burial of a Bear and Child From the Sacramento Delta", in Institute of Archaeology, University of California Los Angeles Journal of New World Archaeology, Vol 1, Number 2, December 1975, 25-30.

De Lys, Claudia. *A Treasury of American Superstitions.* New York: The Philosophical Library, 1948

Dickman, Henry. "Treatment of Diseases by Charms as practiced by the Singalese in Ceylon" in *Transactions of the Ethnological Society of London, Vol. II.* London: John Murray 1863

Elworthy, Frederick Thomas. *The Evil Eye: The Classic Account of an Ancient Superstition.* Mineola: Dover Publications, Inc. 2004

Evans, E.P. *Animal Symbolism in Ecclesiastical Architecture.* London: W. Heineman 1896

Frankfurter, David. "Healing Spells" in Meyer, Marvin W. and Richard Smith, ed. *Ancient Christian Magic.* Princeton: Princeton University Press 1994

Gamst, Frederick C. *The Qemant: A Pagan-Hebraic Peasantry of Ethiopia.* New York: Holt, Rinehart and Winston Case Studies in Cultural Anthropology 1969

Gimbutas, Marija. *The Language of the Goddess.* San Francisco: HarperSanFrancisco 1991

Gimbutas, Marija. *The Civilization of the Goddess: The World of Old Europe.* San Francisco: HarperSanFrancisco 1991

Granger, Byrd Howell. "Some Aspects of Folk Medicine among Spanish-speaking People in Southern Arizona" in *American Folk Medicine A Symposium.* Berkeley: University of California Press 1976

Grant, Campbell. *Rock Art of the American Indian.* New York: Promontory Press, 1967

Green, Miranda. *The Gods of the Celts.* Glouchester: Alan Sutton 1986

Greenwood, Susan. *The Encyclopedia of Magic & Witchcraft.* London: Hermes House 2005

Guiley, Rosemary Ellen. *The Encyclopedia of Witches & Witchcraft.* New York: Checkmark Books/Facts on File 1999

Hand, Wayland D. *Magical Medicine.* Berkeley: University of California Press, 1980

Hopkins, E. Washburn. *Epic Mythology.* Delhi: Motilal Banarsidass 1986

Hopper, Vincent Foster. *Medieval Number Symbolism: Its Sources, Meaning, and Influence on Thought and Expression.* Mineola: Dover Publications, Inc. 2000

Howells, William. *The Heathens: Primitive Man and His Religions.* New York: The Natural History Library/Anchor Books 1962

James, E. O. James, E.O. *The Ancient Gods.* Edison: Castle Books 2004

Jones, David E. *Sanapia: Comanche Medicine Woman.* New York: Holt, Rinehart and Winston Case Studies in Cultural Anthropology, 1972

Kehoe, Alice B. and Thomas F. Kehoe. *Solstice-Aligned Boulder Configurations in Saskatchewan.* Canadian Ethnology Service Paper No. 48. Ottawa: National Museums of Canada, 1979

Keister, Douglas. *Stories in Stone.* New York: MJF Books 2004

Kieckhefer, Richard. *Magic in the Middle Ages.* Cambridge: Cambridge University Press 1989

Köiva, Mare. "Palindromes and Letter Formulae: Some Reconsiderations" in *Folklore*, Vol. 8, December 1998. Published by the Institute of Estonian Language, Tartu

Lamont-Brown, Raymond. *Scottish Folklore.* Edinburgh: Birlinn Limited, 1996

Mackenzie, Donald A. *Myths and Legends: India.* London: Studio Editions 1985

Mackenzie, Donald A. *Ancient Man in Britain.* London: Senate 1996

Maxwell-Stuart, P.G., editor and translator. *The Occult in Mediaeval Europe.* Hampshire: Palgrave MacMillan 2005

McGowan, Charlotte. *Ceremonial Fertility Sites in Southern California: San Diego Museum of Man Papers No. 14.* San Diego: San Diego Museum of Man, 1982

Merrifield, Ralph. *The Archaeology of Ritual and Magic.* New York: New Amsterdam Books 1987

Meyer, Marvin W. and Richard Smith, ed. *Ancient Christian Magic.* Princeton: Princeton University Press 1994

Michell, John. *Megalithomania.* Ithaca: Cornell University Press, 1982

Mooney, James. *Myths of the Cherokee.* New York: Dover Publications, Inc. 1995, 306. A reprint of the 1900 publication "Nineteenth Annual Report of the Bureau of American Ethnology, 1897-98.

Mooney, James. *The Ghost Dance Religion and the Sioux Outbreak of 1890.* Chicago: University of Chicago Press 1965

Oakes, Lorna and Lucia Gahlin. *Ancient Egypt.* New York: Barnes & Noble, Inc. 2006

Ogden, Daniel. "Binding Spells: Curse Tablets and Voodoo Dolls in the Greek and Roman Worlds" in *Witchcraft and*

Magic in Europe; Ancient Greece and Rome. Philadelphia: University of Pennsylvania Press 1999

Ogden, Daniel. *Magic, Witchcraft, and Ghosts in the Greek and Roman Worlds.* Oxford: Oxford University Press 2002

Opler, Morris Edward. *An Apache Life-Way: The Economic, Social, and Religious Institutions of the Chirichaua Indians.* Chicago: University of Chicago Press 1941

Paine, Sheila. *Amulets: Sacred Charms of Power and Protection.* Rochester: Inner Traditions 2004

Parler, Mary Celestia. *Folk Beliefs from Arkansas, Vol 3.* Fayetteville: University of Arkansas, 1962

Parrinder, Geoffry. "The Witch as Victim" in *The Witch in History* edited by Venetia Newall. New York: Barnes & Noble 1996

Randolph, Vance. *Ozark Magic and Folklore.* New York: Dover Publications, Inc. 1964

Rands, Robert L. "Some Manifestations of Water in Mesoamerican Art," Anthropological Papers, No. 48, Bureau of American Ethnology Bulletin 157. Washington: Smithsonian Institution 1955

Rhys, John. *Celtic Folklore: Welsh and Manx.* New York: Gordon Press 1973

Roberts, A.H. "We Aren't Magicians, But...Verbal Charms Survive in the Machine Age" in *Tennessee Folklore Society Bulletin, number 18, 1952*

Ross, Anne. *Folklore of the Scottish Highlands*. Gloucestershire: Tempus Publishing Ltd. 2000

Russell, Jeffrey Burton. *Witchcraft in the Middle Ages*. Ithaca: Cornell University Press 1972

Silverberg, Robert. *Mound Builders of Ancient America: The Archaeology of a Myth*. Greenwich: New York Graphic Society Ltd., 1968

Simpson, Jacqueline and Steve Roud. *Oxford Dictionary of English Folklore*. Oxford: Oxford University Press 2000

Simpson, Jacqueline. "Evil eye," in *Medieval Folklore*. Oxford: Oxford University Press 2002

Spence, Lewis. *Legends and Romances of Brittany*. Mineola: Dover Publications, Inc., 1997

Spence, Lewis. *The Magic Arts in Celtic Britain*. Mineola: Dover Publications, Inc. 1999

Spier, Leslie. *Yuman Tribes of the Gila River*. New York: Dover Publications Inc., 1978

Thomsen, Marie-Louise. "Witchcraft and Magic in Ancient Mesopotamia" in *Witchcraft and Magic in Europe: Biblical and Pagan Societies*. Philadelphia: University of Pennsylvania Press 2001

Thompson, C.J.S. *The Hand of Destiny: Everyday Folklore and Superstitions.* London: Senate 1995

Tresidder, Jack. *Symbols and Their Meanings.* London: Duncan Baird Publishers 2000

True, D.L., C.W. Meighan & Harvey Crew. *Archaeological Investigations at Molpa, San Diego County, California.* University of California Publications in Anthropology, Volume 11, Berkeley: University of California Press, 1974

Viluoja, Eha. "Manifestations of the Revenant in Estonian Folk Tradition", in Folklore, Vol. 2.
http://www.folklore.ee/folklore/vol2/viluoja.htm 8/14/06

Walker, James R., ed by Elaine A. Jahner. *Lakota Myth.* Lincoln: University of Nebraska Press, 1983

Weir, Anthony and James Jerman. *Images of Lust: Sexual Carvings on Medieval Churches.* London: Routledge 1993

Whiting, Beatrice Blyth. *Paiute Sorcery: Viking Fund Publications in Anthropology Number Fifteen.* New York: The Viking Fund 1950

Wilbert, Johannes. *Yupa Folktales.* Los Angeles: Latin American Center, University of Los Angeles, 1974

Wilde, Lady. *Irish Cures, Mystic Charms & Superstitions.* New York: Sterling Publishing Co., Inc. 1991

Wilkinson, Richard H. *The Complete Gods and Goddesses of Ancient Egypt.* Lonson: Thames and Hudson Ltd. 2003

Index

A

Africa, 12, 43, 51, 73, 90, 123, 144, 163,166
Ainu, 51, 52,
amber, 121, 157, 158
American River, 140
amulets, 6, 7, 9, 10, 12, 13, 17, 20, 21, 28, 29, 30, 31, 35, 43, 48, 55, 66, 67, 73, 81, 104, 106-109, 111, 116, 119, 156-163, 168, 169, 171, 173,
Apache, 53, 55, 70, 95, 96, 99, 107, 108, 109, 126, 127, 145
Australia, 69, 113, 143, 144, 149
Aztecs, 102, 123, 157, 167

B

Babylon, 11, 66, 88, 119, 166
bear, 51-58, 104, 109, 123, 139, 143
bewitchment, 15, 71
burning, 13, 18, 24, 29, 62, 71, 100, 147

C

cairns, 136, 140
California, 18, 55, 56,57, 123, 124, 140, 141, 143, 157
Canada, 52, 63, 159, 168
cat, 51, 58-66, 102, 113
Celtic, Celts, 14, 26, 42, 55, 67, 68, 72, 89, 93, 101, 102, 121, 148, 151, 166
charm wand, 27
charms, 6, 9, 13, 14, 17, 19, 20-25, 28, 29, 30, 36, 43, 60, 65, 94, 102, 104, 111, 112, 117, 118, 119, 156, 159, 160, 161, 162, 173
Cherokee, 69, 95, 96
Cheyenne, 86
children, 9, 12, 13, 14, 17, 20, 26, 58,, 59, 61, 66, 95, 96, 108, 112, 121-124, 126, 129, 132, 133, 137, 152, 157-160, 162, 172
Christian, Christianity, 6, 9, 21-23, 25, 28-33, 35, 40, 54, 60, 65, 71,

72, 74-77, 81, 82, 83, 84, 88, 89, 94, 117, 118, 125, 130, 150, 153, 154, 168-170
Christian magic, 28-33
clootie, 163-165
coins, 159, 170-172
copper, 98, 159
coral, 156, 158, 159
Cornwall, 132, 133, 137, 151, 164, 165
cosmic egg, 76, 98, 99
creation, 82, 83, 91, 139, 166, 173
Crete, 79, 85
crippled, 17
cross, 18, 21, 30, 64, 75, 84, 89, 94, 113, 116, 160, 166, 168, 169
cunning men, 31
cuse tablets, 36-39, 111
curses, 12, 18,, 31, 36, 37,38, 39, 40-42, 67, 83, 111
Cyprus, 37, 40

D

daggers, 43, 44, 45, 48
deformed, 16, 18
demons, 10, 26, 28, 29, 33, 35, 48, 50, 65, 78, 80, 92, 117, 134, 162
Devil, 11, 28, 34, 54, 62, 79, 115, 136, 148, 149, 151, 162, 163

dogs, 17, 31, 53, 61-65, 113, 156
dragons, 48, 77, 79, 86, 88, 92

E

Egypt, 9, 12, 17, 19, 25, 27, 31, 38, 59, 65, 66, 67, 91-93, 116, 122, 126, 158, 159, 161
elderly, 16, 17
England, 36, 38, 60, 61, 64, 65, 68, 71, 72, 77, 132, 141, 149, 152, 153, 158, 162, 163, 165
Ethiopia, 15, 118, 129
Euphrates river, 23, 88
evil, 3, 6, 12, 13, 14, 16, 20, 25, 29, 32, 33, 35, 42-44, 48, 50, 54, 60, 63, 65, 71-74, 76, 77, 91, 94, 95, 100, 106, 111, 119, 121, 126, 130, 132, 157, 161-163, 165, 171
evil eye, 10, 11-20, 27, 121, 158, 160, 162, 171

F

Faery, 53, 132, 148, 151
familiars, 21, 28, 61, 71
fertility, 14, 30, 55, 66, 69, 76, 78, 87, 92, 93,

106, 107, 122-126, 128, 158, 161, 166
figurines, 85, 106, 110, 160
flood, 97, 140
folk-medicine, 17, 64, 157, 158, 168
foot snake, 96
frogs, 17, 26, 41, 51, 62, 66-73, 133

G

Germany, German, 25, 47, 64, 126, 160, 171
geysers, 55
Gnostic Christians, 83, 84, 89
god, goddess, 6, 10, 12, 14, 20-22, 25, 28, 31, 35, 37, 39, 48, 51-68, 70, 73-83, 85, 88-95, 97, 101-106, 110, 111, 116, 119, 123, 127, 130, 135, 142, 150, 151, 153, 158, 160, 167, 169-171, 173
Great Basin, 70, 124
Greece, Greek, 17, 22, 25, 28, 36, 40, 42, 52, 61, 67, 78, 79, 82, 84, 85, 89, 90, 93, 111, 117, 126, 129, 153, 158
green, 91, 92, 119

H

healing, 25, 31, 47, 68, 89, 90, 119, 127, 132, 134, 136, 137, 138, 140, 146, 153, 154, 155, 157, 158, 159, 164
healing wells, 164
heaven, 76, 78, 84, 91, 102, 145, 160, 166, 168
Hebrides, 141
Hecate, 61, 66
herbs, 21, 29, 30, 43
horns, horned, 17, 78, 88, 97, 101, 102, 104, 105
horseshoes, 13, 14, 23, 25, 161, 162
Hupa, 141, 143, 144

I

illness, 14, 28, 31, 32, 35, 43, 51, 53, 96, 108, 111, 119, 121, 129, 130, 134, 136, 140, 146, 147, 154, 156, 157, 159, 164
incantations, 14, 23, 24, 29, 35, 36, 84, 111-114, 116, 117, 118, 144
India, 12, 58, 78, 80, 87, 88, 127, 133, 158
Iowa, 98

Iran, 72, 79, 80
Ireland, 93, 94, 121, 136, 137, 139, 143, 146, 164
iron, 13, 14, 23, 33, 48, 50, 138, 161

J

jade, 102, 123, 158
jaguar, 60, 70, 102, 103, 110
Japan, 51, 59, 144

K

kolossi, 111
kris, (weapon) 48, 49, 50

L

Lakota, 55, 94, 132, 152, 181
lead tablets, 36, 40, 111

M

madstone, 156
magic, 10, 12, 14, 20, 21, 25, 26, 27, 28, 29, 30, 31, 32, 40, 43, 45, 48, 54, 61, 62, 66, 77, 81, 93, 102, 105, 110, 111, 113, 116, 117, 118, 120, 130, 134, 136, 144, 152, 159, 165, 168, 169
magic wand, 25, 26

May cats, 61
Mayan, 60, 68, 69, 87, 103, 166
meander lines, 77, 87, 143
Mesoamerica, 60, 68, 70, 82, 86, 87, 89, 166, 167, 168,
Mesopotamia, 12, 78, 88, 102, 111
Mexico, 12, 14, 102, 107, 157
Miwok, 56, 57
Mongolia, 53, 70, 158, 164
mountains, 25, 51, 52, 94, 96, 107, 120, 122, 127, 148, 153, 164

N

Nahuatl, 168
Native American, 55, 57, 86, 87, 89, 94, 97, 100, 104, 107, 109, 110, 113, 139, 140, 152, 164, 166, 168,
Northstar stone, 56
Northumberland, 130, 164
Norway, 72, 147

O

offering, 68, 84, 102, 125, 132, 159, 164, 165, 171

Ohio, 18, 64, 86, 98, 121, 134
Oregon, 64, 112
Otherworld, 77, 86, 129

P

pagan, 6, 9, 21, 25, 28, 30, 31, 33, 40, 74, 81, 94, 100, 118, 125, 130, 142, 143, 168, 170
Paiute, 111
Palomar Mountain, 144
Plains Indians, 57
poor, 17, 26, 64, 96
prayer, 28, 29, 30, 32, 38, 40, 52, 118, 126, 166

Q

Qemant, 15, 118
Quetzalcoatl, 82, 123, 166, 167, 168

R

rabbit feet, 162
rain, 59, 60, 61, 64, 68, 69, 86, 87, 94, 95, 97, 108, 109, 115, 139, 141, 143, 144, 145, 167
rain rocks, 57, 139, 143, 144
Reformation, 32, 33

religion, 22, 28, 29, 32, 38, 40, 50, 51, 54, 57, 66, 70, 76, 83, 88, 92, 101, 104, 111, 116, 142, 168
ritual, 6, 13, 29, 30, 31, 32, 35, 40, 41, 44, 51, 56, 64, 67, 84, 86, 95, 100, 102, 103, 110, 111, 119, 125, 127, 129, 130, 133, 134, 136, 139, 141, 144, 148, 149, 154, 158, 163, 168,
rock art, 47, 70, 77, 86, 143
Roman, 12, 17, 36, 61, 66, 67, 79, 80, 115, 117, 120, 126

S

Sacramento, California, 57, 140, 175
sacrifice, 29, 60, 65, 68, 79, 84, 100, 171
San Diego, California 144
Sancreed, 164
Scotland, 14, 77, 121, 129, 133, 136, 145, 151, 154, 164
serpent, 17, 26, 73, 74, 75, 76, 77, 78, 79, 80, 81, 82, 83, 85, 86, 87,

88, 89, 90, 91, 92, 93, 95, 97, 99, 100, 101
serpent gods, 85, 90, 92, 93
Serpent Mound, 86, 98
serpent-men, 80, 81
shaman, shamanism, 26, 40, 43, 53, 55, 56, 70, 95, 102, 104, 108, 110, 118, 127, 139, 143, 144, 152, 158
shape-shift, 53, 55, 62, 110, 114
snake, 22, 25, 26, 61, 68, 70, 73, 76-79, 82, 83, 85-91, 94-99, 101, 102, 110, 117, 138, 156, 158, 159
snake-dragon, 88
sorcerer, 10, 37, 111, 112, 114, 118
spells, 6, 9, 10, 20, 22, 23, 28, 29, 30-32, 36, 37, 38, 40, 42, 68, 111, 112, 113, 115, 117, 118
springs, 38, 76, 145
St. Nectan, 164
standing stones, 119, 125, 129, 139, 141, 148, 151
steel, 47, 48
stone, 6, 13, 14, 35, 42, 56, 65, 70, 73, 80, 82, 86, 94, 98, 106, 107, 110, 119-156, 158, 160, 173
superstition, 29, 61, 71, 98, 128, 159
Sweden, 65, 94
swords, 29, 47, 48, 50, 53

T

talisman, 6, 14, 17, 154, 156, 160
Tennessee, 95
thunder god, 76, 94, 95
Titans, 80, 81
toads, 66-73, 110
tortoise, 69
totems, 51-104
tree, 16, 24, 30, 53, 54, 75, 78, 87, 89, 97, 127, 143, 158, 163-166, 171
Turkey, 164
turquoise, 108, 109
Twelve Tables, 111, 115

U

Underworld, 40, 53, 55, 57, 60, 61, 63, 778, 80, 102, 109, 147
Ur, 88

W

Wales, 41, 147
wands, 25-17, 63

weapons, 32, 43, 44, 45, 47, 49, 50, 109, 159
wells, 38, 40, 72, 132, 133, 134, 138, 141, 143, 146, 159, 163, 164, 165, 171
Wiccan, 25, 27, 161
wind, 61, 64, 76, 77, 86, 132, 141, 145, 146, 166
wise women, 31
wishing wells, 164, 171
witch, witchcraft, 6, 10, 11, 13, 14, 15, 17, 19, 23, 24, 30, 31, 33, 35, 36, 38, 40, 42, 43, 50, 60, 61-66, 68, 71, 112, 114, 118, 122, 130, 133, 139, 146, 161, 162, 169
witch bottles, 23
women, 9, 13, 15-17, 21, 26, 31, 36, 48, 51, 58, 64, 122, 124, 125, 127, 129, 130, 133, 151, 153, 166
word-square, 22, 23

Gary R. Varner

About the Author

Gary R. Varner has written several books and numerous articles on folklore, mythology, ancient traditions and contemporary issues. His articles have appeared in international journals, such as the British magazine on holy wells and waters, *Living Spring Journal* and the German periodical, *Magister Botanicus*. His books have delved into sacred wells and holy waters, the Green Man, gargoyles and ancient iconography, Native Americans, mysterious creatures and megalithic sites around the world, among others. He is a member of the American Folklore Society as well as the Foundation for Mythological Studies.

Readers are invited to visit the author's website at www.authorsden.com/garyrvarner.

Made in the USA
Lexington, KY
08 June 2018